Consciousness of Artistic Form

by Henry Schaefer-Simmern

First Edition
Published in the United States of America by:

The Gertrude Schaefer-Simmern Trust
2014 Norwood Drive, Carbondale, IL 62901
Phone: (618) 549-3471

Editor: Gertrude Schaefer-Simmern
Assistant to the editor: Roy E. Abrahamson, EdD
Historical drawings: Sylvia Fein
Book design & production: Massey Design Associates, Berkeley, California
Printer: Malloy Incorporated, Ann Arbor, Michigan

Library of Congress Cataloging-in-Publication Data

Schaefer-Simmern, Henry, 1896-
    Consciousness of artistic form : a comparison of the visual, gestalt art formations of
children, adolescents, and layman adults with historical art, folk art, and aboriginal art / by
Henry Schaefer-Simmern ; editor, Gertrude Schaefer-Simmern ; assistant to the editor, Roy
E. Abrahamson ; historical drawings by Sylvia Fein.
      p. cm.
    Includes bibliographical references and index.
    ISBN 0-9742039-0-4 (hc. : alk. paper) — ISBNN 0-9742039-1-2 (pbk. : alk. paper)
      1. Art, comparative. 2. Figure-ground perception. 3. Creation (Literary, artistic, etc.)
I. Schaefer-Simmern, Gertrude. II. Abrahamson, Roy E. III. Fein, Sylvia. IV. Title.

N7428.5.S33 2003
701—dc22
                                                                              2003064241

CONSCIOUSNESS OF ARTISTIC FORM

A comparison of the visual, gestalt art formations of children, adolescents, and layman adults with historical art, folk art, and aboriginal art. Supporting the theory of a unifying art-forming ability that is universal, timeless, and cross-cultural.

By Henry Schaefer-Simmern

Editor:
Gertrude Schaefer-Simmern

Assistant to the Editor:
Roy E. Abrahamson, EdD

Historical drawings:
Sylvia Fein

Wild Animal in a Jungle Pool

Sarah, age 8 years, painted this picture of a wild animal standing in a jungle pool, surrounded by trees and plants. The animal, colored reddish brown, is set off clearly from the ground area of the pool with its blue color. In turn, the figure of the pool also takes on figural meaning, set off clearly by the beige, tan color of the jungle with its reddish trees with green foliage. Sarah is on a more advanced level of the primary stage of figure-ground relationships, therefore. She is also on the stage of unified direction of figures, and on a more advanced level of the early stage of color usage than that of many primary grade level children. Note how Sarah indicated hair on the animal with waving red lines, and showed ripples in the pool with wavy dark blue strokes.

This book is the product of Henry Schaefer-Simmern's lifelong research of art works from 40,000 years of history. *The hundreds of examples included here support his belief that we have an inherent consciousness for artistic form and that this has existed in the human mind as far back as we have any record. Schaefer-Simmern also proposed that artistic form will develop naturally if children are not influenced by the demands, expectations, or rules of well-meaning adults who usually have little or no knowledge of the artistic process. With adult interest, however, and appropriate tools, children's artistic development will follow identifiable stages that involve basic art elements and their relationships.*

At each stage of artistic form development, from the simplest scribbles to complicated configurations, a comparison will be made of children's, adolescents' and adults' art works with folk art, aboriginal art, and ancient art. Through descriptions, examples, and comparisons, readers can gain a sound understanding of the inherent process of visual conceiving and its artistic, gestalt form as a process (and ability) that most human beings appear to have regardless of factors like race, sex, socio-economic status, geographic location, time, and so on.

This book is dedicated

to the memory of

Henry Schaefer-Simmern

and his wife,

Gertrude Schaefer-Simmern

CONTENTS

ACKNOWLEDGMENTS

The following people helped make this book possible:

Professor Henry Schaefer-Simmern, the author of the original material, who gathered visual art examples from many historical periods and places for over 40 years and who passed away before he could finish writing the text. Now the book is completed, based on lecture notes, recordings, and other sources true to his theory and teachings, and it is indeed the culmination of his life's work that he began in pre-war Germany, and brought into full fruition in his adopted homeland of the United States.

Dr. Egon Kornmann, foremost student and follower of Gustaf Britsch of Germany. After Britsch died, Kornmann and Britsch's widow, Luise, directed the Gustaf Britsch Institut für Kunstwissenschaft und Kunsterziehung in Starnberg, south of Munich, Germany. Just prior to this death, out of his considerable respect for Schaefer-Simmern's research and teachings, Dr. Kornmann kindly agreed to write the foreword to this book. (Professor Schaefer-Simmern had based portions of his theory of artistic visual conceiving upon Gustaf Britsch's theory of artistic consciousness.)

The Editor, Mrs. Gertrude Schaefer-Simmern, widow of Henry Schaefer-Simmern, being familiar with her late husband's theory, research and teachings, first undertook to finish this book. In addition, she funded the work, and after her death late in the year 2000, her estate continued to fund the efforts made to complete this book.

Assistant to the Editor, Roy E. Abrahamson, EdD, a former full-time student of Professor Schaefer-Simmern's at the latter's Institute of Art Education, in Berkeley, Calfornia, was asked by Gertrude Schaefer-Simmern to help her to complete this book. Abrahamson, a former public school teacher in San Francisco, California, who later earned his doctoral degree at Teacher's College, Columbia University, under Dr. Edwin Ziegfeld, was then a professor of art education (now retired) at Southern Illinois University, Carbondale, Illinois. A former president of the Illinois Art Education Association, he presented papers at numerous conferences of the National Art Education Association, and at international congresses of the International Society of Education through Art, and also published articles in professional journals on various aspects of Schaefer-Simmern's works.

Sylvia Fein, who made hundreds of the fine pen and ink drawings of historical, aboriginal, and folk art included in this book. A known painter and author, she was impressed while reading Henry Schaefer-Simmern's book, *The Unfolding of Artistic Activity*, and subsequently met him at his Institute of Art Education. She developed a relationship of true dedication as a student at the Institute, and for years since that time assisted Schaefer-Simmern on the initial work for this book. Her two books, *Heidi's Horse* and *First Drawings: Genesis of Visual Thinking*, were both dedicated to him.

Kerwin Whitnah, artist, art teacher and former layman student of Henry Schaefer-Simmern, who anglicized the translation of the German text of Dr. Kornmann's foreword for this book. After having studied at the Institute of Art Education, Kerwin, who died in 1999, proved to be a dedicated supporter of Professor Schaefer-Simmern, arranging lectures for, and speaking on behalf of the latter.

Ruth Dyer, a relative of the late Gertrude Schaefer-Simmern, and executrix of the latter's estate. Miss Dyer did much to support the completion of the book during its rewrite, design and printing phases, working closely with Dr. Abrahamson, and Gertrude Schaefer-Simmern's attorney, Mr. Ian McPhail.

Ian McPhail, Attorney at Law in Aptos, and Carmel, California. He served as Gertrude Schaefer-Simmern's attorney during her life in Carmel, and he continued to act as attorney of the Gertrude Schaefer-Simmern Book Trust after her death. Mr. McPhail has worked closely with Dr. Abrahamson and Miss Dyer to make possible the final form of this book. His wise suggestions are much appreciated.

Massey Design Associates, under the direction of Mr. John Massey, of Berkeley, California, have done a highly professional job of bringing the manuscript into a readable, well-designed form, coordinating all efforts with the Assistant to the Editor, the Executrix of the Estate, and the Attorney of the Trust.

Marianne Abrahamson, who gave Dr. Abrahamson many helpful suggestions and showed great patience during the long developmental phases of this book.

"The life and work of Henry Schaefer-Simmern covers decades of my own work and life. And it would take much more than a page to reflect some of it.

But, having reached almost a century of my own life and work, to which Henry contributed so much, I must limit myself to recommending the addition of Henry's work whole heartedly."

Rudolf Arnheim
Professor Emeritus
Psychology of Art

FOREWORD

Henry Schaefer-Simmern was gifted with two outstanding qualities: first, his natural ability as a teacher, and second, a deep insight into the nature of the mental process which produces artistic formations. At a very early stage in his career he understood clearly that mere conceptual thinking or intellectual inquiry does not lead to the natural unfolding which the true artist must undergo if he is to generate artistic structures from the chaos of the visual world. He grasped an essential insight: "All primordial thinking takes place in terms of images."(1948) Thus he was able to build a pedagogical theory which accurately described the process of *visual thinking* as of primary importance in the artistic process. His often repeated dictum sums up this point of view: "What is not born in vision through the process of visual conceiving cannot live as artistic form."

Schaefer-Simmern was deeply aware that we live in a time of great difficulty for the visual arts. He knew that 200 years of mass produced artifacts had imposed a mechanical and non-artistic restraint on man's innate capacities. Through intense study of past epochs and close examination of the art produced by children, naive painters, and modern primitives, he was able to guide his students to a sure grasp of the artistic form as brought forth by their own effort and tested by intuitive self-criticism.

Henry Schaefer-Simmern's deep dissatisfaction with the styles and fads of art and art education led him to discover the seminal work of Gustav Britsch who died in 1922. Britsch, through long research and experimentation, had conclusively demonstrated that the *genuine* drawings and paintings of children are determined by inherent laws of consciousness which unfold in a succession of logical "steps" or progressive mental levels of pictorial realization. Thus, the child who is gifted and protected in his unfolding is able to produce unified and simplified configurations out of the multifarious and confusing abundance of the visual world.

The present work is both a supplement to and a magnification of Schaefer-Simmern's highly esteemed book, *The Unfolding of Artistic Activity*, first published in 1948 with a foreword by John Dewey.* It gives in-depth treatment to the concepts first presented in that volume and provides voluminous illustrations of the artistic form as it evolves from the simple to the complex in many epochs and strata of society. This important work sums up a particular thrust of the achievements of art education in the Twentieth Century and builds a sure foundation for future research and actual classroom practice. It is the crowning (though posthumous) achievement of one of the most gifted and dedicated art educators of our time. (Note 1)

Egon Kornmann

*Now in its fifth printing by the University of California Press, Berkeley

Egon Kornmann was Gustaf Britsch's foremost student and disciple, and for many years after Britsch's death directed the Gustaf Britsch Institut für Kunstwissenschaft und Kunsterziehung in Starnberg, south of Munich, West Germany. Henry Schaefer-Simmern sought and received suggestions from Kornmann from time to time in regard to the manuscript on which this book is based.

PREFACE

This book presents artistic forms,* or gestalt formations, as revealed in the visual art of prehistoric and historic, aboriginal, and folk artists as well as in the art of contemporary children, adolescents, and lay adults. Henry Schaefer-Simmern gathered evidence of artistic forms over many years in order to demonstrate the existence in human beings of a consciousness for conceiving of such forms according to an inherent artistic ability. Due to his death in October 1978, however, his manuscript was left unfinished. Material from it, illustrated by hundreds of his collected images, forms the basis for this work.

In order to place the book in proper perspective, a brief biography is provided here.

Born in Haan, Germany, in 1896, Henry Schaefer-Simmern studied as a young man to be a teacher and also, upon the death of his father, to be an artist. He became a member of Das Junge Rheinland, an organization of artists that included Otto Dix and Max Ernst. He taught art in a town, Simmern, near the Rhine River and later added the town's name to his own because art critics had been confusing him with another Schaefer. While teaching in Simmern, he was struck by the close relationship between the folk art of the Rhine Valley and the art of his rural students. Thus he began to formulate a theory of artistic consciousness that he called "visual conceiving." The main hypothesis of his theory is that inherent in the human mind is the ability to transform perceptual experiences into gestalt formations of images and groups of images that are expressed as works of art. He believed that even children have such an ability on a simple level.

Later, as a professor at a college in Frankfurt am Main and while conducting research with unemployed workers, Schaefer-Simmern attended, on behalf of the newspaper *Frankfurter Zeitung*, an international congress on art education in Prague. There he heard a presentation on Gustav Britsch's theory of artistic consciousness by Egon Kornmann. Schaefer-Simmern was greatly impressed by Britsch's theory, which in its fundamental aspects was similar to his own developing hypothesis. He built upon Britsch's theory as he continued his research with children, adolescents, college students, and the unemployed. Because the Third Reich was becoming increasingly totalitarian and oppressive, however, he emigrated to the United States in 1937. He taught himself to read and speak English and eventually obtained a grant from the Russell Sage Foundation of New York City to conduct research with juvenile delinquents, developmentally disabled women, refugees, and professional people. His book, *The Unfolding of Artistic Activity* (Schaefer-Simmern 1948), contains reports on this research.

His research with developmentally disabled women at Southbury Training School in Connecticut in the 1940s has been acclaimed by psychologists, mental health experts, art therapists, and art educators throughout the world. It was observed by

---

This term is equivalent to gestalt art forms, which consist of holistic structures in which the basic art elements (lines, shapes, spaces, and so on) are interfunctionally related to each other and to the whole. These artistic, gestalt forms are created in the mind's subconscious, intuitive domain and are expressed through tools, materials, processes (drawings, painting, etc.), and techniques as works of art.

Seymour B. Sarason, noted psychologist, who was on the Southbury staff at that time. One can read Sarason's account of the research with Selma, one of Schaefer-Simmern's subjects, in *Psychological Problems in Mental Deficiency* (Sarason 1949, 316-321) and *Psychology and Mental Retardation* (Sarason 1985, 123-143).

In addition to publication of his own book, Schaefer-Simmern, with Fulmer Mood, translated from the original German and published *On Judging Works of Visual* (Fiedler 1949) by Konrad Fiedler, a little-known German philosopher. A close friend of Adolf Hildebrandt, the sculptor, and Hans von Maree, the painter, Fiedler (1841-95) lived and worked in the Munich area. His philosophy of art formed the basis for both Britsch's and Schaefer-Simmer's theories, although certainly they arrived at some concepts in their own ways. Herbert Read, the British writer and art historian, believed that Fiedler's notion of the existence of a form of artistic cognition that was just as valid as abstract, conceptual cognition, was of fundamental importance. He dedicated his book, *Icon and Idea* (Read 1955), to Fiedler and quoted extensively from Fiedler's *On Judging Works of Visual Art* in his own *The Forms of Things Unknown* (Read 1960, 39-43).

After teaching as a visiting professor at the University of California in Berkeley for a few years, Schaefer-Simmern established his Institute of Art Education in that city in 1949. He taught and conducted research at the Institute with everyone from children to student teachers and artists. He also conducted research at various community centers in the Bay Area.

In 1955 he published *Sculpture in Europe Today* (Schaefer-Simmern 1955) after obtaining and organizing photographs of leading European sculptors. Later he participated in a symposium on children's art held on the Berkeley campus, and his presentation, "The Mental Foundation of Art Education in Childhood," was included in a symposium report published as *Child Art: The Beginnings of Self-Affirmation*, edited by Hilda Present Lewis (Lewis 1966, 47-68).

Schaefer-Simmern joined the faculty of St. Mary's College of California in Moraga in 1961 and taught there until he retired in 1978. A short time later he was awarded the honorary doctor of humane letters degree by the college's board of trustees. On October 16 of that year, Henry Schaefer-Simmern passed away.

A brief description of the hypotheses of his research will be helpful here to see the relationship between his concern for evidence of artistic form and the main aspects of his theory of visual conceiving.

1. We are born with an inherent, lawful process of visual conceiving according to which perceptions of our environment are transformed into gestalt formations called *artistic forms* and expressed with tools, materials, and other means as art works, no matter how simple.

2. These artistic forms unfold and develop from simple structures of lines, shapes, and spaces in young children's art to the increasingly complex artistic forms that may be produced by adolescents and adults.

3. While visual conceiving functions interactively with one's physical, social, and cultural environments, it is an autonomous process insofar as it operates beyond

the dictates and limitations of our psychomotor, affective, and cognitive domains. During the process of visual conceiving, however, these domains function in the service of the visual conception and artistic, intuitive cognition and thought.

4. The person in whom visual conceiving is active tends to function as a psychobiological whole and, over a period of artistic activity, may experience a form of unification and clarification that beneficially affects the whole being.

5. Since visual conceiving is an inherent human attribute, evidence of its artistic forms can be found in visual art produced by children as well as adults from all historical periods.*

With regard to this last hypothesis, Schaefer-Simmern did not believe, or state, that all things made by people and called art have been, are, or will be visual, artistic conceptions having artistic forms. He knew full well that numerous influences and interferences may partially or completely stifle the process of visual conceiving in any person or group. For example, the *laissez-faire* approach doesn't challenge students to evaluate their art and thus develop their inner sense for unity of artistic forms. Academic approaches such as discipline-based art education fail to bring forth students' senses for artistic forms because they impose rules and methods that interfere with the natural stages of development.

Schaefer-Simmern did not ignore cultural influences, but the works that he necessarily focused on showed positive cultural influences that allowed for the free expression of inherent artistic conceptions. His research, like that of Britsch and Kornmann, showed clear evidence of developmental stages in terms of figure and ground (Note 2), line, shape, and directional relationships. The various levels of unfolding were compared in contemporary prehistoric, historic, aboriginal, and folk art.

Some art educators mistakenly identified Schaefer-Simmern's ideas with the theory of recapitulation, which had been disproved earlier, and therefore dismissed them. According to that theory, formulated by Ernst Haeckel, the 19th century German biologist, each animal passes through the stages already gone through by its evolutionary ancestors (Encyclopedia International).

For more than 50 years, Henry Schaefer-Simmern conducted research in art museums, galleries, libraries, and other sites in Europe, the United States, and elsewhere in order to gather visual evidence of artistic, gestalt forms in art. This book reveals the results of his years of patient research in art of all the ages.**

---

* *"Henry Schaefer-Simmern: His life and Works," Roy E. Abrahanson, Art Education, the journal of the National Education Association (NAEA), (December 1980, v. 33, no. 8, pp. 12-16); and "The Teaching Approach of Henry Schaefer-Simmern," Roy E. Abrahamson, Studies in Art Education, the quarterly research journal of the NAEA, (1980, v. 22, no. 1, pp. 42-50).*

**Certainly not all of the artworks that Schaefer-Simmern examined possessed artistic form: the degrees ranged from lack of artistic form to partial artistic form to complete artistic form. It is safe to say that the art that became a part of his research collection fell within the range of the second and third categories. He did refer in his teachings to the first category, however, and showed examples to his students.*

INTRODUCTION

What do we mean when we speak of "a work of art?" It is a monument to the human spirit that is represented by the artistic consciousness of the human mind and its ongoing process of unfolding and development of artistic cognition. This book is dedicated to the light of artistic consciousness that exists in children, adolescents, and adults; in the art of naive artists, folk artists, and aboriginal artists; and that reaches out to us from prehistoric and historic art throughout the world.

To create a work on any level that can rightfully be called art, there must be an intense visual experience involving intuition, clear perception, honest judgment, and keen deliberation. Among the impediments to such an experience in our "new millennium" culture are the artificial distractions of a child's everyday life (television, comic books, advertisements, movies, computer games, and other mass-market distractions) and the scarcity of worthwhile art programs. Children's visual experiences today are heavily influenced by a chaotic environment that conflicts with their own genuine conceptions.

It is now very difficult to find a drawing or other art work done by older children in this country that contains artistic, gestalt form. Poor or absent art education programs stifle their inherent artistic conceptions, and those schools in which art is taught advocate a conceptual, cognitive systems learning approach or a type of self-expression that provides no opportunities for artistic growth. The chief objective of those who advance the former approach seems to be the teaching of prescribed concepts, formulas, methods, and techniques so that students will acquire conceptual knowledge about art and, in some cases, produce visual statements (drawings, painting, etc.) by following the steps taught to them. Although advocates claim that creativity still has value in art education, there is little time for it in a program in which so much adult-prescribed, body-of-knowledge material is taught. In the latter approach, few, if any, art concepts are developed, and no means for self-improvement is given. Stages of development identified by responsible researchers of children's art are ignored, if not condemned.

Sadly, the present emphasis does not encourage children or adults to create their own artistic conceptions of the visible world. Indeed, even in elementary school many children have already begun to doubt the value of their own art and to copy the art of others. A second-grade teacher who had her pupils make valentines from white lace paper and red paper recently complained that, unlike the kindergartners, many of her children were unable to create their own art. When all of their finished valentines were taped to a wall, nearly half of them were seen to be copies of one that she had shown to the class.

This teacher coincidentally mentioned another interesting point: younger children seem blessed with their own insulation from adult interference with their creative art. Even if they have an adult's picture or design in front of them, they make their own art. Their artistic conceptions—so clear and strong that hardly anything can block them— survive in spite of our mechanized, intellectualized culture. Certainly young children need some guidance even though they have this clear artistic vision. Teachers need to help them with tools, materials, processes, and from time to time they need to be challenged. Possible courses of action can be suggested and questions can be asked to evoke their powers of observation, comparison, and decision making.

However, it is the older children and teenagers who especially need assistance. Many need to be guided to regain artistic attunement and need assurance that their own genuine artistic conceptions are valid and appreciated. Their education requires a balance between the unfolding and expression of their own artistic abilities, on the one hand, and the impact of facts, formulas, and figures from their culture on the other hand. However, their own artistic vision should play a leading role in attaining this balance.

Teachers need to base their approach upon each student's visual ability to evaluate his or her art works and upon awareness of the process of visual conceiving and artistic formation. Artistic activity cannot begin where educators impose on students externally formulated images and methods, concepts and cognition. A transaction between the individual and his or her physical, psychological, and social environments is necessary for true artistic activity. The artist in whom visual conceiving is active needs to express the mental artistic forms in order to become more conscious of and understand them as art objects. He or she needs, in short, *to become conscious of consciousness* within and emanating from the being. In doing so, the physical, affective, and cognitive domains of his or her being function in coordination with and in service to the artistic process.

Artistic form, that is, a holistic structure or unity of parts within a whole (gestalt) has been expressed for ages past, regardless of canons of art, rules, religious laws, or other cultural devices or influences. Where no artistic form can be seen in objects that some call "art" of the past, it can be assumed that cultural pressures or influences prevented its existence. In this book, we present evidence to support the hypothesis that an inherent consciousness for artistic, gestalt form exists in the human mind and in art born of that consciousness. Never before in the English language has artistic form been more fully demonstrated. The book is the product of Henry Schaefer-Simmern's life-long research into art collected from 40,000 years of history. At each stage of artistic form development, childrens', adolescents' and lay adults' art works are compared with folk art, aboriginal art, historic art, and prehistoric art to demonstrate the universal laws of artistic vision.

Close inspection of these examples provides insights into the precision, wisdom, logic, inventiveness, and even playfulness of the artist as well as ideas about the origin and development of artistic form and its arrangement into increasingly complex gestalt formations. The pictorial evidence is identified as to origin and, whenever possible, date. Descriptions and comparisions are made through either photographic or accurate pen-and-ink drawing reproductions.

As the Table of Contents shows, the stages of development deal with basic art elements and their relationships. Because the clearest and most common of these are *line* and *angle-of-line* relationships, they are given primary attention. They range from early spiraling and circular or oval images through horizontal-vertical line relationships and variable line relationships. Other stages of development deal with *figure-ground* relationships, *spatial orientation* of images, and the *direction* of similar images in pictorial space. Various ways of showing direction and distance or depth and a thorough examination of depictions of the human head and face are presented. The book concludes with a chapter on the recommended teaching approach.

Through the description, examples, and comparisons, we hope to provide a sound understanding and appreciation of the inherent process of visual conceiving and its artistic, gestalt form as a process, and ability, that most humans appear to have regardless of race, sex, age, socioeconomic status, geographic location, and time.

CHAPTER ONE

From Scribbles to Circular Images

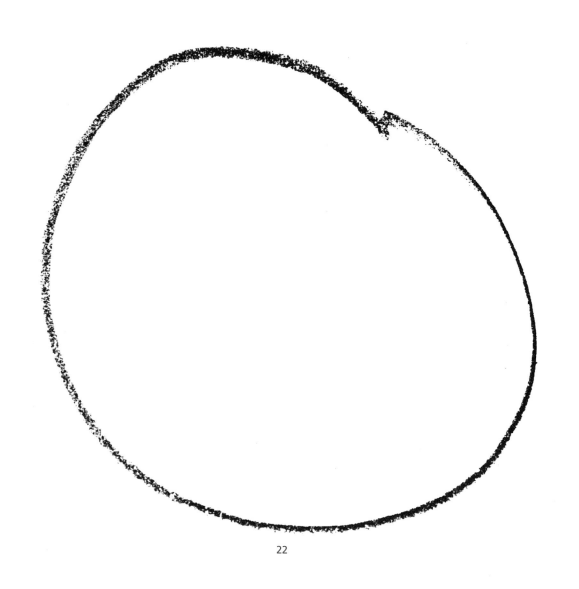

2

1

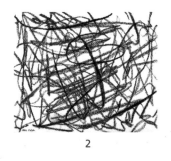

2

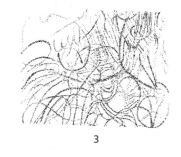

3

4

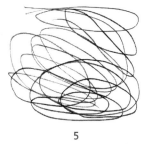

5

6

A momentous experience occurs when a child first grasps a pencil or crayon and sees that it makes a mark when moved across a piece of paper—something appears on the paper that was not there before. It is not only the image itself that is momentous but the fact that it is the result of the child's tool manipulation. These first scribbles have little, if any, structural pattern, and various shapes or line directions (straight, coiling, curved, or zigzag) may appear in any one of them (figs. 1 and 2). Dictated by the movements of the shoulder and arm joints and muscles, they may be made for many months before the appearance of the "organized" scribble (figs. 4 and 5), where we see that the movement is mostly circular. The children who made these have gained more muscle control as well as more skill in using their pencil or other marking tool.

Similar behavior can be observed in prehistoric art. From the Early Stone Age, around 40,000 B.C., in France, Spain, Germany, Italy, Malta, and China, we have visual evidence of early man's artistic development. Fig. 3, a finger engraving from Paleolithic France, is an exact counterpart of fig. 2, and fig. 6 mirrors figs. 4 and 5. Artistically, a child can be said to be a contemporary of early artists. That is, the child and the early artists express the same visual artistic forms. (Please note that we won't speculate about possible cultural, religious, or other symbolic meanings of past art. We are only interested here in the visible facts—the artistic form of lines, shapes, spaces, and so on.)

Figs. 7 and 8 show how order begins to evolve from scribbles. At first this happens simply by virtue of the child's increasing coordination and dexterity: for example, the straighter lines are no longer accidental. (Figs. 9-11 show prehistoric artists at a similar stage.)

7

8

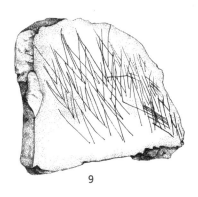

9

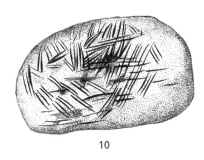

10

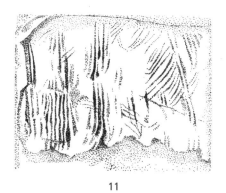

11

12

13

14

15

16

17

18

19

20

FROM SPIRALING TO CIRCULAR IMAGES

At around three or four years of age, a rudimentary spiral, or coiling, system may appear in children's drawings (figs. 12-14). There is empty space around their figures, and they are aware of the paper's edge. They have more control over, and more confidence in, their own bodies now. They are also more visually aware and are beginning to make basic artistic judgements. Figs. 15-18 are ancient examples, and 19 and 20 illustrate how the spiral image was used in tombs and on pottery, jewelry, weapons, utensils, and monuments.

While the spiral image is evident for a time, gradually fewer and fewer coiling lines appear, until the line is turned across itself and a circular or oval shape appears. Using the circular* image (figs. 21-24), their first outlined or enclosed shape, children of three or four describe their worlds. At this early stage, the meanings assigned to their images may change from hour to hour. "Mama" may become "choo choo" later in the day. Although the natural appearance of these subjects is obviously very different, children's visual configurations aren't influenced by such complications. Figs. 25 and 26 show the same circular images in historic artworks.

In the 1920s, the anthropologist Hugo Bernatzik discovered a tribe in the remote jungles of Thailand, the Phi Tong Luang, who had neither houses nor beds and lived in a round ditch below ground level. When Bernatzik gave some of these people crayons and paper, to his amazement, they drew only circular images. When asked what the images represented, the tribespeople would say, "This is a jaguar. This is a bird. This is a god. This is my grandfather." The circular image repre-

*Because the circle is an adult geometrical concept, the author preferred to describe this form in children's art as "evenly extended and directed." However, we will use "circular" for convenience.

sented every one of these subjects to them. The anthropologist had discovered a tribe of people whose level of visual conception was identical with that of very young children.

The author did not ask children to define or title their images, because he believed that if they were forced into thinking about objects abstractly and conceptually, their natural development would be harmed. Neither should parents and teachers tell children what to draw. By watching and listening, he thought, they would gain insights from the artwork about what children might be thinking and feeling about the work and other matters. He did encourage adult interest, help with providing proper tools, and sometimes even intervention. For example, he believed that, when tired, children sometimes revert to an earlier stage in their artistic development. If they have been busily drawing or painting with circular forms and revert to spirals or scribbles, he recommended that their parents or teachers interrupt and say, "That's enough for today."

When children are frustrated by their need to solve a visual problem, they often display great power and determination that lead to a successful and sometimes intricate solution. They seem to recognize the necessity of carrying the artwork through from start to finish; that is, the beginning determines the end. In mathematics, this is called logic; in art it is called *consciousness of artistic form*.

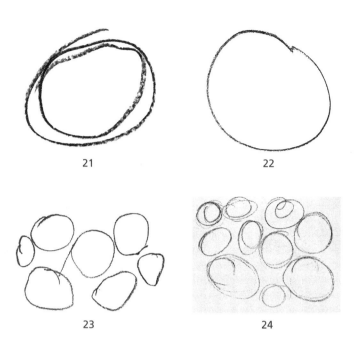

21   22

23   24

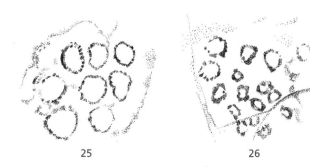

25   26

FIGURE AND GROUND

When children place their first scribble completely on the paper—not allowing it to wander off onto the table or floor—they show their dawning visual awareness of figure and ground relationships. The image of all those coiling lines, for example, takes on what in Gestalt psychology has been called "figural" meaning, and the surrounding blank paper takes on "ground," or pictorial background, meaning. First with the spiral image, then with the circular, the figure/ground relationship becomes more firmly fixed in children's minds.

The figure and ground relationship is the fundamental factor for all future artistic conceptions. The figure, or image, cannot exist without the surrounding, or ground, that sets it off by contrast; the ground has no meaning without the figure. (Note 3) (See Chapter 5 for more on this topic.)

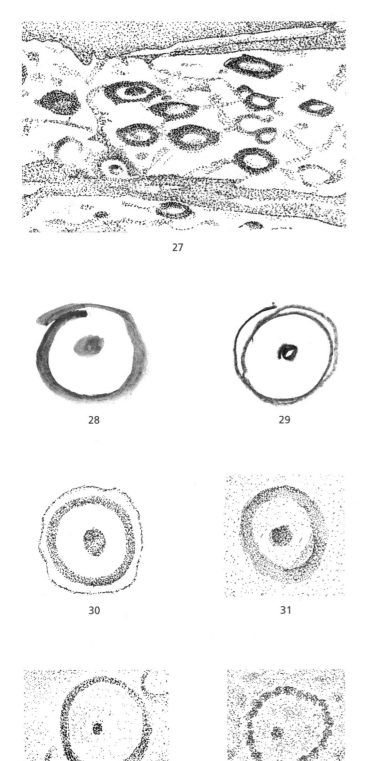

27

28

29

30

31

32

33

CONCENTRIC AND NONCONCENTRIC CIRCULAR IMAGES

The mind does not stand still. After children have been at the circular stage for awhile, naming one such image "Mama," for example, and another image in the same drawing "Papa," they discover that they can create something new by placing a small circle inside a larger one. This new formation gives them an additional and slightly different image to which to assign meaning. For example, Mama can be shown by the more complex circular image and Papa by the simpler one.

Since the outline of a single circular image makes a powerful visual impression on children, they will attempt to make the smaller circle as parallel to the first as possible. They may even place a still smaller image inside the second one and so on.

As for the spatial relationships between figure and ground, the empty space on the paper surrounding the first circular form sets off the first, larger image. The empty space between the first image and the smaller one inside it serves as a ground area that sets off the smaller image. On the child's part, this is a subconscious, visually intuitive process. (Note 2)

The images appear not only in children's art but in historical art as well. The children's images (figs. 28 and 29) and the historical art (figs. 27, and 30-33) show the very beginning of concentric images, and figs. 34-36 show these images as used by children between the ages of 3 and 7. Figs. 37-41 show reversions to the concentric stage in more advanced artistic forms.

34

35

36

37

38

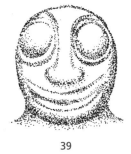

39

40

41

Eventually children begin to embellish their circular images by adding several nonconcentric circular images inside the original large figure (figs. 42 and 43). The need to create concentric images lessens as they explore this addition of non-parallel images inside a large circle or oval. Their use of concentric circular images there vanishes but may reappear later in parts of more complex images. In "Cat with Kittens," smaller shapes are placed in this particular way. In "Many People in a House," the house and people are indicated in the same way, but the people are within the outlined figure that is the house. Such drawings are done by children everywhere. Sometimes these figures are meant to be automobiles in a garage, children in a classroom, animals in a cage, and so on.

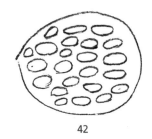

42

43

ARTISTIC COGNITION

It is important to remember that artistic visual conception does not deal with the reproduction of viewpoints but with an intuitive visual understanding that we call "artistic cognition." So children who have the ability for visual conception are concerned with the creation of relationships in the realm of artistic vision. They show their own clearest conceptions of what they see. When they are not influenced into thinking they should copy or imitate, they are stimulated by their perceptions, whether of nature or of manmade objects, and are not disturbed by their complexities. They transform their perceptions, subconsciously or intuitively, into their own holistic conceptions, and they use only those aspects of what they see that are important to them and that can be "fused" with their stage of artistic development.

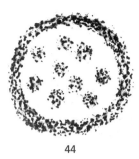

44

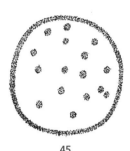

45

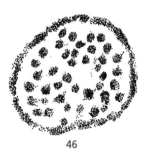

46

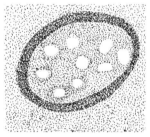

47

It is probably worth mentioning here something that teachers and others who work with groups of children know: not all children follow the same path from one stage to another. Some may move abruptly to the next stage; others may skip a stage entirely. Most children, however, hold onto some aspects of the earlier stage before they step completely into the new.

CIRCULAR IMAGES AND SUBJECT CONTENTS

Those children who have never seen a horse have little idea of a horse. What a child does with any subject in his or her art depends on individual mental and artistic vision. While outside perceptual stimulation is necessary for children and even older people who are engaged in artistic activity, in the early stages there is no need to be very concerned about this: children cannot at this point produce forms that are developed enough for us to see a relation to objects in their environment.

We can see the same forms from prehistoric times (figs. 44-47) and can assume that the same artistic laws were at work then as now. (Our visual understanding of many ancient art works is improved if we free ourselves from the habit of seeing from a single viewpoint [e.g., "side view," "front view," etc.]. These works become comprehensible if we can see their gestalt or near-gestalt forms and realize that they represent the prehistoric or ancient artists' clearest visual conceptions.)

More evolved images can be seen in figs. 48-53. In fig. 48, the outer circular image is Mama, and the inner shapes are parts of her new dress. Fig. 49 is a similar drawing by an older developmentally disabled child, and figs. 50-53 are examples created by early man.

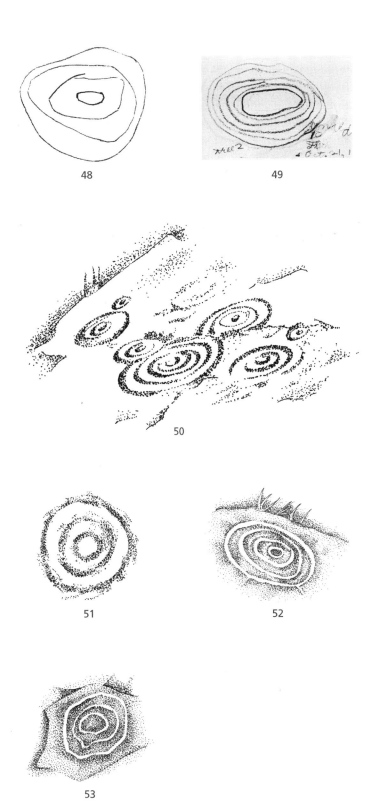

48

49

50

51

52

53

54

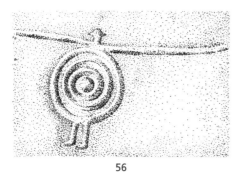

55

REVERSION TO CONCENTRIC CIRCULAR IMAGES

The complex body of the person in fig. 54 does not show intestines, as one might suspect, but instead the child's expression of a coat and buttons, which he could not yet form. He doesn't engage in conceptual, abstract thinking; instead he intuitively organizes the whole by using circular images within circular images. The same is true for fig. 55. (Both of these figures illustrate how circular images can be combined with horizontal and vertical lines, but we will pursue this stage in the next chapter.) Historical examples in figs. 56-58 illustrate the logic and inventiveness of ancient artists, while figs. 59-62 are again of young children's drawings. Figs. 63-69 depict artistic expressions from many countries and periods. (Note 7)

56

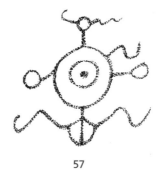

57

58

59

60

61

62

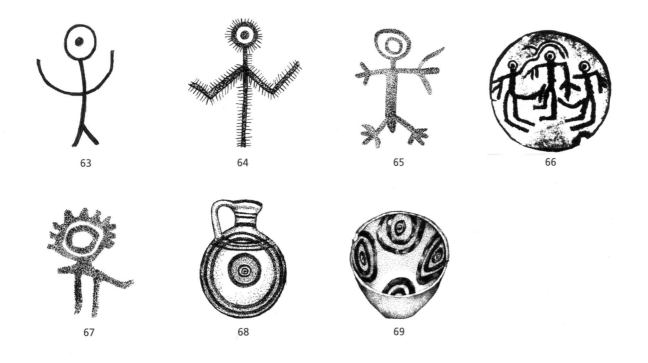

63 64 65 66

67 68 69

In fig. 70, we see in the child's idea of a flower the same concentric images, and figs. 71 and 72 show each child's conception of "tree." The trees were not drawn imitatively but according to the children's own artistic conception; they were understood visually through their circular images.

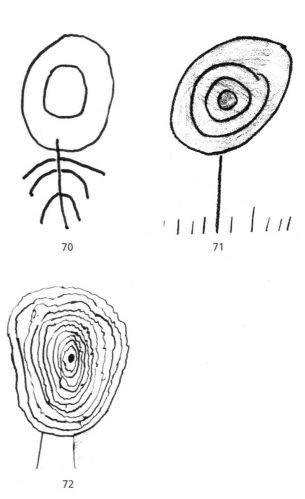

70 71

72

75

73

74

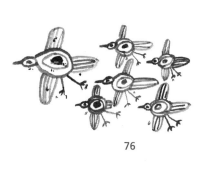

76

77

78

79

80

The inner circular forms indicate fruit or leaves. Figs. 73-75 are examples of historic and ancient artists' works on a similar level of development, and figs. 76-80 show such reversions in animal and bird images.

Spontaneously and intuitively, children express the order that occurs when their perception of an object is transformed into the visual conception that they can best understand. The tree image is one child's visual conception of a tree that he has seen. He doesn't analyze the tree—he creates. Most great artists operate in the same manner, transforming the external environment into their own visual conceptions. Children, too, have this unsullied creative ability within themselves.

THE SMILING MOUTH

Sometimes only parts of concentric shapes are necessary (fig. 81). The head-face is circular, and Willy has fitted in the eyes and nose. But when he came to the mouth, he felt the urge to repeat a circular shape within the circular shape of the face and drew a second curved shape parallel to the first. The naïve viewer might say, "This is a drawing of a smiling face." But this is not so. Willy adhered to his visual understanding of the concentric circular image, and the mouth simply follows the circular outline of the face.

Fig. 82 is another example of this configuration, except that Paula used only one curved, partially concentric line for the mouth. In "Somebody Hung Himself" (fig. 83), a man is hanging by his neck from a rope attached to a tree limb. There is no smile in this unhappy portrayal—simply a mouth that curves in parallel conformity to the circular image. Fig. 84 is a fine example of a cat drawing that shows the same configuration in the cat's mouth.

This basic stage of development is found in the beginnings of art of all races. Figs. 85-89 show historical examples from different countries and times. They and figs. 81-84, 90, and 91 illustrate what art historians call the archaic smile, because it is not what it seems. (The term refers to the smile typical of Greek sculpture of the Archaic Period. The rather grim "smile" may have resulted from the technical difficulty in fitting a curved mouth shape in the block-like head of the sculpture of that time [Encyclopedia Britannica].)

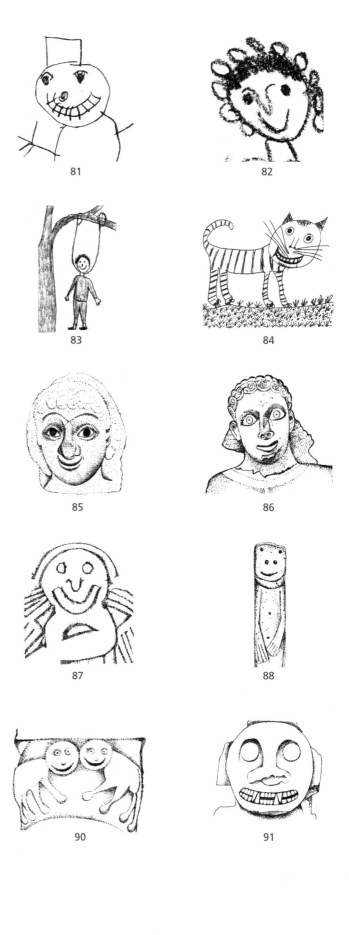

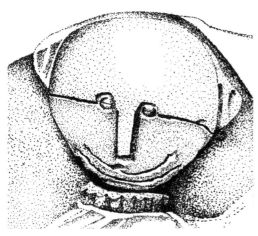

89

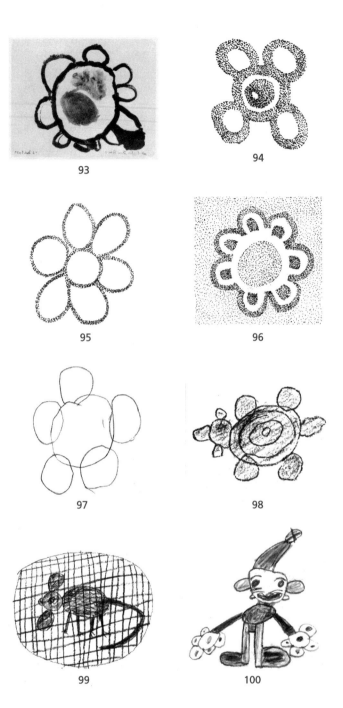

93

94

95

96

97

98

99

100

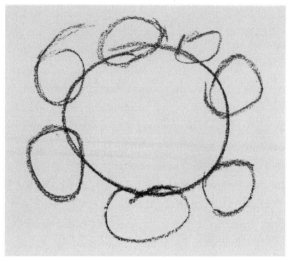

92

SURROUNDING AND TOUCHING CIRCULAR IMAGES

The following examples show the diversity in different children's drawings and ancient artists' paintings and rock engravings. Figs. 92 and 93, "A Ball with Wheels On," demonstrate again how children use only the symbols that are on the levels of development they have achieved. Historical figs. 94-96 illustrate the same stage of conception, as does the perfectly organized drawing entitled "A Flower" (Fig. 97), which could have meant and been named anything else, at a different time, by its creator. The intricate pattern of the shell of Clement's "big turtle" (fig. 98) is indicated with concentric circular images, and in Paul's "A Mouse in a Trap" (fig. 99), an outlined circular figure with intersecting lines represents the trap. The body of the mouse is circular, as are the large ears, head, and nose. The eye is a large dot placed directly in the middle of the head, and even the tail is a half-circular shape. In "A Clown" (fig. 100), Stephen made a cluster of circular shapes in the clown's hands.

Figs. 101-107 are historical examples of the diverse uses of the circle. (Sometimes older children and even adults revert to this early form, using it to surround more complex images.)

101

102

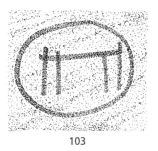

103

104

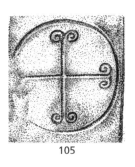

105

106

SUMMARY

We have explored the basic development of artistic forms in children's art through examples that show spirals and circular and concentric forms arising out of the earliest scribbles. Their development is compared to that of prehistoric man and artists of other ages and locales. We have introduced the importance of the figure-ground relationship, which will be pursued in more detail in Chapter 5. Much of the chapter has been devoted to circular images and their variations, and in Chapter 2 we will see how these are combined with straight lines and directional shapes at the next developmental stage.

107

CHAPTER TWO

Horizontal-Vertical Line Relationships

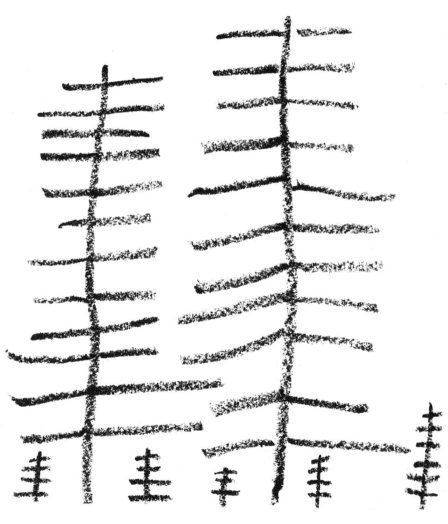

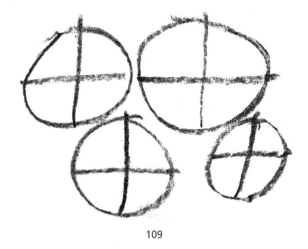

109

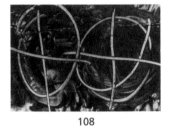

108

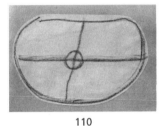

110

Between the ages of approximately three and six years, most children are content to draw circular and concentric circular images. But their minds grow, and finally they must do something more. They begin to discover new relationships—relationships that are not found in nature but that are stimulated by nature. For some children, this discovery comes quite early: the circular shapes with two crossed lines (figs. 108-110) were done by three- and four-year-olds. It seems as if, using these lines, they seek to confirm what the author termed the "evenly extended and directed" nature of the form: the crossing point of the lines emphasizes the center of the circle. (Historical and prehistoric examples are shown in figs. 111-116) More lines follow: some pointing toward the center and others radiating from the center toward the circular outline and beyond. These new structures develop from the previous primary forms in an organic fashion. (Note 4)

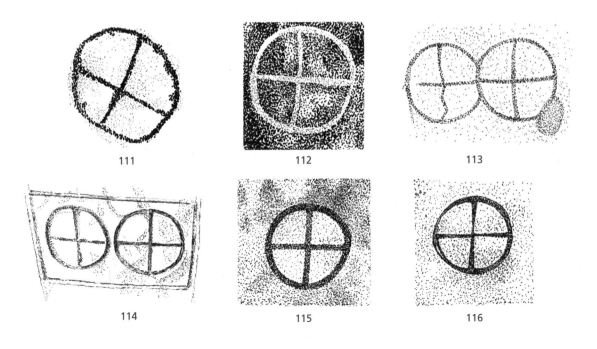

111

112

113

114

115

116

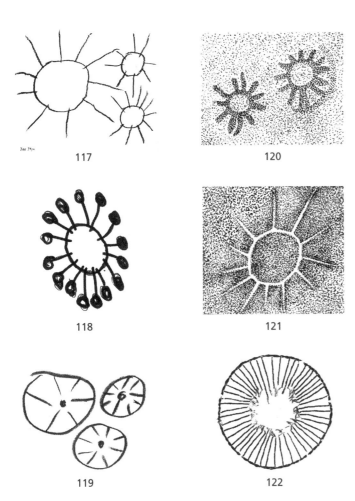

117

120

118

121

119

122

THE BEGINNING OF HORIZONTAL-VERTICAL LINE RELATIONSHIPS

Figs. 117-119 are further examples of circular images with radiating lines done by children of about three years of age. The nearly perfect order that occurs is deliberate. As the radiating lines touch the circular outline at nearly right angles, a new configuration is created—the horizontal-vertical*—that will determine children's direction in artistic growth for many years. Early man was apparently guided by the same artistic impulse, and there are additional examples (figs. 120-122) from prehistoric Spain, South Africa, and North America.

Children express this newfound relationship in different ways (figs. 123-125), and it is interesting to compare these to the rock engravings of ancient artists (126-128). The circle-like image with radiating lines has a direct visual impact. It is a universal symbol that occurred during the Bronze Age of most peoples. The examples in figs. 129-130 by young children are almost perfect

*Another of the author's terms for this configuration was "greatest contrast of direction."

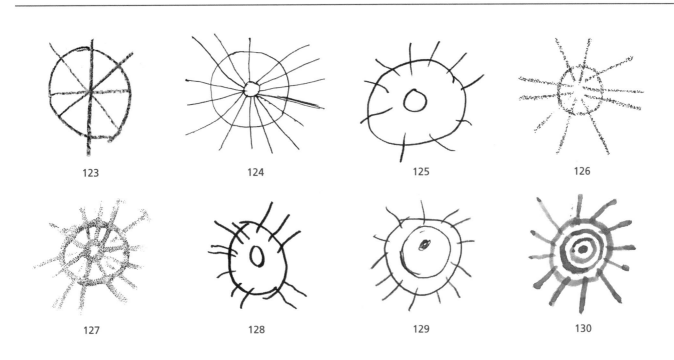

123

124

125

126

127

128

129

130

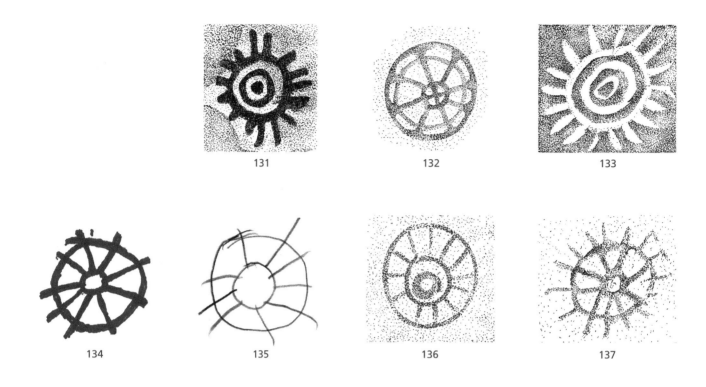

131

132

133

134

135

136

137

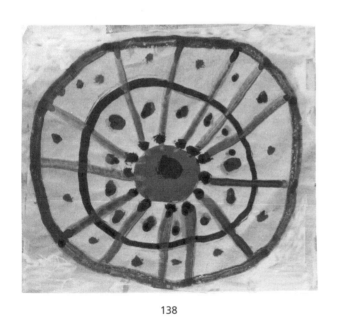

138

139

counterparts of figs. 131-133 by early people. Figs. 134-135 and 136-137 likewise show similarities between preschool children's and early people's drawings. Fig. 138, done by a young child, and fig. 139, from 6th century Palestine, show complex forms like those in figs. 134-136.

Radiating lines touching the circular figure are the first indication of the new line-and-angle relationship that leads to the full horizontal-vertical stage in children's artistic cognition. (Note 5) A group of nursery school children's drawings (figs. 140-144) shows only a limited number of radiating lines and a variation of the horizontal-vertical relationship. Figs. 145-148 show historical examples of the same stage.

144

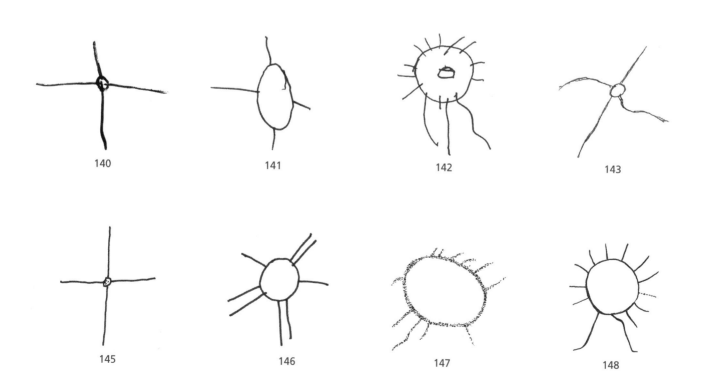

140 141 142 143

145 146 147 148

149

150

151

152

153

154

155

156

157

A nursery school child's idea of the human figure (fig. 149) illustrates how the vertical direction of the form, rather than any particular personal attributes, has precedence at this stage, but other drawings by children between the ages of three and five (figs. 150-157) begin to show the dominant features—eyes, nose, mouth, arms, and legs. The "man" in fig. 150 is a circular image with concentric circular images, two vertical lines extending into the outer circle, and two short vertical lines attached to the smallest circle. This child has learned that radiating lines, formerly used to indicate legs, can be replaced by parallel lines for the same purpose. (The shorter lines may indicate hair.) In his depiction of a man, Tom used radiating lines that begin at and extend outward from the circular outline (fig. 151). The small circles within the larger one stand for eyes, nose, and mouth. The radiating lines in fig. 152, however, are drawn from the outside toward the center of the circle and may represent hair.

As the human face is one of children's earliest visual and psychological experiences, and as the circular primeval form stands for their first visually fixed idea (indeed, the first structure that they can grasp mentally), it is often disproportionately large. Children don't remember Mama, Daddy, or Uncle Richard by their big feet or hands. If we think of someone, we visualize first of all his or her face, and so it is with a child. It would be wrong to suppose that children intend to draw legs or arms fastened to the head or arms coming out of the legs. At this early stage, they don't draw what they know intellectually and neither do they draw what they perceive. Instead, the stage of their visual conceptions and artistic cognition governs how they draw people and other objects from their environments.

In fig. 153, both arms and legs extend from the outline of the circle in the greatest contrast of direction (i.e., they are approximately perpendicular to the circle). The legs, however, are parallel to one another and do not extend from the circle's radius, as the arms do, but from points on the circumference that made visual sense to the

158

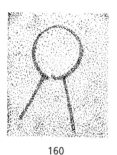

159

160

161

162

163

artist. Fred's friends' legs show the same parallelism (fig. 154), as does the person drawn by Henry (fig. 156). However, Henry's arm lines are in full horizontal-vertical relationship to the leg lines and therefore show a more advanced stage.

But let us consider a puzzling phenomenon. Why do all of the "friends" in fig. 154 look alike? It is because children at this stage operate with a very basic idea: people are people. They understand the outlined figure of a person, and they understand the structure of the face. They could do a whole battle scene with people in simple linear relationships. But they are not yet aware enough of the differences among faces and their features to express them artistically. From the art of the Romanesque Period to that of the great masters of 14th century Europe, the angels look alike—whether French or German or Italian —as if they too were all brothers and sisters. Only a very general face is visually grasped at first; details and differentiation come much later.

Four radiating lines emerge from the head in fig. 155, illustrating how the strength of this relationship lingers in the four-year-old's mind. In figs. 156 and 157 two five-year-olds at a later stage have drawn fingers radiating from circular hands. The structure of the latter drawing is roughly similar to the first but indicates a "body." The historical and more modern examples of adult images in figs. 158-164 are not exact counterparts to the children's drawings but demonstrate an identical stage of visual conception. (Note 5)

164

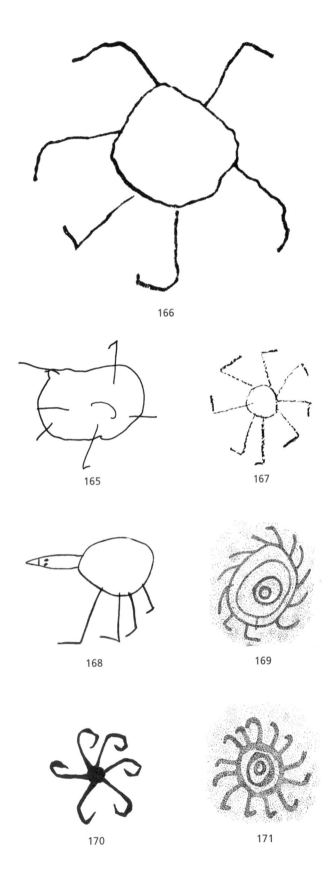

166

165

167

168

169

170

171

EXTENSIONS OF THE NEW LINE RELATIONSHIP

A structure that often appears in children's artwork between the ages of two and five resembles a swastika. (The swastika shape is an ancient, primeval symbol that was used in Sumeria around 5000 B.C., in China around 2500 B.C., by native North and South Americans, and by many other ancient peoples.) To children it often represents something that is moving, perhaps because it suggests turning or spinning, like a pinwheel. Figs. 165-168 were described by their creators as a train locomotive, a many-legged man, a jumping calf, and a horse.

The previous examples, as well as those from the history of art (figs. 169-171) show how children and ancient artists progressed from the early realization of horizontal-vertical line relations to the full horizontal-vertical stage. We can't refer to the extensions in their drawings (figs. 165-167) simply as "feet," although they serve as such in figs. 166 and 167, because they may carry other meanings. Certainly the locomotive has no feet. (Note 6)

In fig. 168, however, Claus indeed meant "feet" (or hoofs) in his horse image. His main structure is a circular image with four legs that tend to go toward the center of the circle as they meet the circular outline in the horizontal-vertical relationship. To these Claus added the neck and the head, which touch the body at the same horizontal-vertical angles.

If these children hadn't told us what they meant (figs. 166, 167), we could not know any more about the content than we do when looking at the historical examples in figs. 169-171.

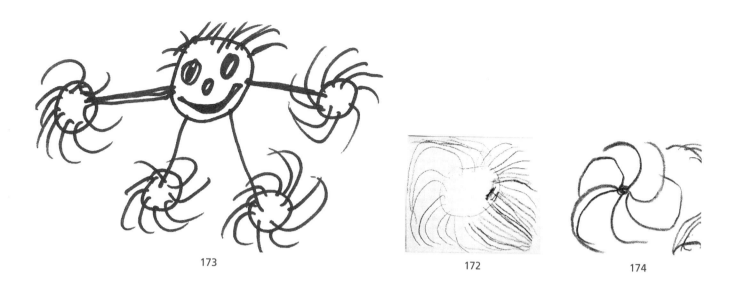

173

172

174

We can only see and comprehend the structure of
lines, spaces, etc. in many early, simple images.
We cannot tell what they represent. The drawings
in figs. 172-174 show variations in the direction
of the lines that appear to radiate from the circular shapes. Instead of abrupt changes of angle at
the extreme ends of the lines (as in figs. 165-167),
they curve in a unified, rhythmic direction.
Circular shapes appear for the eyes and nose in
fig. 173, as well as for the hands and feet. In figs.
169-171 and 175-178, these symbols appear in
images from different periods of history.

175

176

177

178

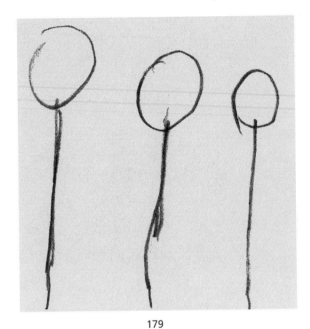

179

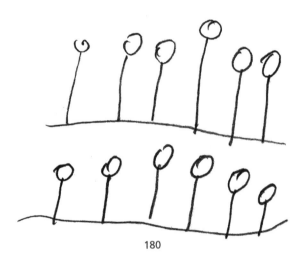

180

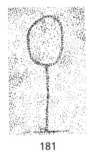

181

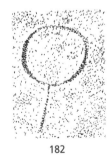

182

EARLY HORIZONTAL-VERTICAL RELATIONSHIPS IN TREES AND FLOWERS

We have studied primarily examples of the horizontal-vertical relationship and directions in children's drawings of the human figure, but regardless of subject the same patterns will be seen. The simple line drawings of figs. 179 and 180 are examples of the nursery school child's first visual conceptions of flowers and trees. A vertical line means "trunk," and the circle attached at the top means "leaves" or "petals." In "Flowers" (fig. 180), the child is still using the circular form to express a variety of ideas or conceptions (also see figs. 181 and 182), but as children's artistic vision develops, they express leaves, branches, stems, and petals in a more complex manner. For example, Karl's radiating lines carry the meaning of "leaves" (fig. 183). Although he was hampered by the big brush that his teacher gave him as well as by dripping paint, the structure of his painting is clear: a vertical trunk joins a circular form. Silvia attached small circles to her radiating lines to show leaves (fig. 184). Now the outside world is beginning to impinge on the child's inner world: more and more details are perceived and transformed in the subconscious and finally combined with the main aspects of a subject. Martin, Billy, Rosalie, and Elizabeth (figs. 185-188) used the same familiar symbols with more differentiation. Fig. 188 is included to illustrate how concentric circles and radiating lines can mean both "eyes" for Elizabeth and a "flower bed" for Rosalie. Figs. 189 and 190 show the work of a folk artist from northern Italy and an ancient Egyptian who were at the same stage as these children.

183

184

185

186

187

188

Children's minds are filled with images. What they depict is not only a reflection of their experiences but also a reflection of their visual understanding at each developmental stage. Artistic cognition (different from, but just as valid as, abstract conceptual cognition) and artistic visual thinking are integral aspects of their mental and emotional existence. At each stage, children conceive and draw (also paint and shape) everything according to their artistic cognition. This is an intuitive, not intellectual and abstract, cognition of the inherent and lawful process of visual, artistic conceiving.

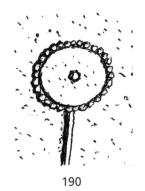

189

190

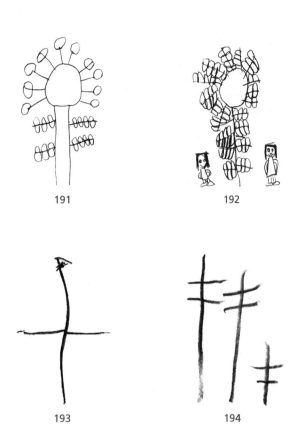

191   192

193   194

A TRANSITION STAGE

After using the circular form with radiating lines for flower and tree images for some time, children may begin to draw or paint branches, stems, and petals in a full horizontal and vertical relationship to the trunk or stem (figs. 191, 192). These transitional examples show both the early horizontal-vertical stage, with lines for branches radiating from a circular tree top, and a more advanced stage where the branch lines are at near right angles to the vertical trunk.

THE FULL HORIZONTAL-VERTICAL STAGE IN TREE AND FLOWER IMAGES

The trees in figs. 193 and 194 show strong horizontal-vertical line directions, and everything that comes to mind visually at this point in children's artistic development is governed by this directional relationship. If they draw a tree in this way (fig. 194), they are soon able to differentiate, but differentiation will be also be governed by the horizontal-vertical. Again we see the same artistic

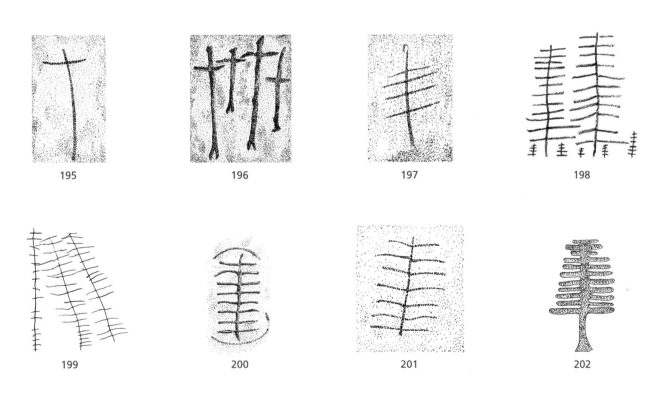

195   196   197   198

199   200   201   202

form in the works of ancient and prehistoric artists (figs. 195-197 and 200-202).

Figs. 198, 199 and 203-205 show five children's simple horizontal-vertical structures. Some of these children have become aware that tree trunks have volume or width: compare the trees in figs. 198 and 199 to those in 203-205. In the last of these, the artist has embellished his picture with birds and flowers. Still, whatever the subject matter, the drawings use only circular shapes and horizontal-vertical directions. Another girl enclosed the branches and leaves of her trees with circular outlines (fig. 206) in order to contain a newly achieved complexity and to clarify her visual conception. A similar but less complex structure is depicted in fig. 207 with only a trunk and main branches, but another child shows leaves, twigs, and secondary branches (fig. 208).

206

203

207

204

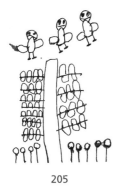

205

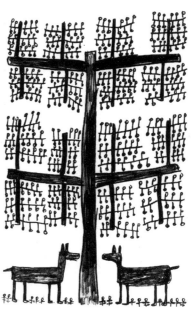

208

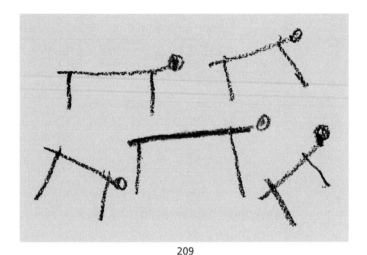

209

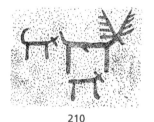

210

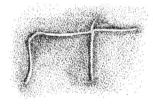

211

212

213

214

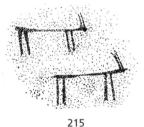

215

HORIZONTAL-VERTICAL IMAGES OF ANIMALS

"Dogs" (fig. 209) shows simple horizontal-vertical structures with circular forms for the heads, but notice that the animals have only two legs. This boy knows that the people around him and he, too, have two legs; therefore, an animal has two legs. He doesn't yet conceptualize and still sees the world in a very general way. (Figs. 210 and 211 are historical examples of similar forms.) The boy who drew fig. 212, "Shepherd Dog," was quite aware, however, that an animal has four legs, as was the Havasupai boy who drew "Three Mules" (fig. 213). Figs. 214 and 215 are historical examples.

Fig. 216, "A Horse," consists of a horizontal line to which seven vertical lines are attached and an irregular oval shape that appears as the head. Each vertical line ends with a tiny circle or oval to denote "foot." This girl knew that the horse did not have seven legs, but either she was compelled by intuition to add more vertical lines to fill the space or she wished to indicate "running." "Dog" (Fig. 217) is structured in the same way as are the historical examples of figs. 218 and 219. (Fig 220 is an example of reversion to circles with radiating lines to show feet.) At this stage, children often draw or paint more than four legs on animals to show that they are running. This effect is also seen in historical example (fig. 222). The inability to draw bent knees or slanted legs and the desire to draw a running figure produce a visually interesting solution—more legs. Many ancient images of running animals done in this way can be wrongly interpreted as "fences" or "combs."

On the "Newspaper Rock" (fig. 223), discovered in Arizona, we can see the same animal structures as we find in the children's drawings. The images on the rock—human as well as animal—make use of the circular forms with radiating lines, concentric circles, and other images and symbols. (Fig. 224 shows an animal done in the same linear way, whereas the animal in fig. 225 has an outlined head, body, and hooves.)

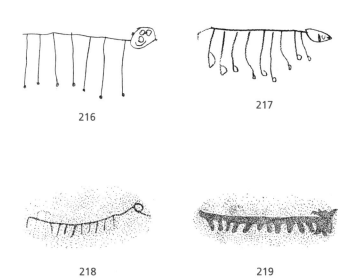

216

217

218

219

Fig. 226 was created by a Havasupai boy who had not yet achieved the fully outlined extension of the animal that would show volume or thickness. The extension is seen in the mules' bodies but not in their legs, which were drawn as continuations of the body lines. This particular figure is also found in early rock engravings (figs. 227 and 228). Heidi's horse (fig. 229) has volume, although only five months earlier this concept wasn't evident in her work (fig. 216). Outlined extensions of bodies drawn by children are also shown in figs. 230 and 231, and the legs in each of these figures (and in fig. 229), while separated from the bodies, are outlined extended rectangles or partial ovals.

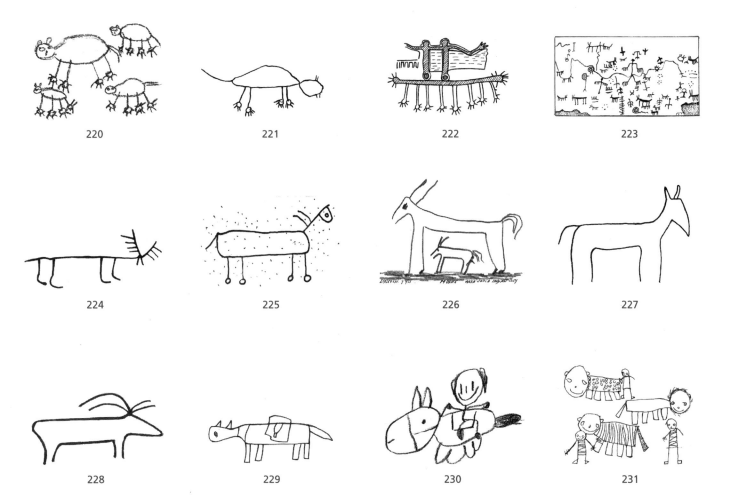

220

221

222

223

224

225

226

227

228

229

230

231

232

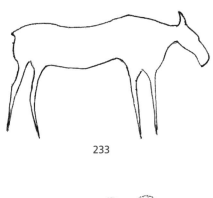

233

234

235

At this stage, most children think in terms of single relationships—everything for itself. Occasionally, however, a child has such a clear visual conception that he or she draws a figure or figures in one line. In fig. 232 is a drawing by a Havasupai boy who lived in a canyon surrounded by high cliffs. Through the clarity of his visual conception, he was able to draw the guide and each horse or mule ascending a trail with one continuous flowing line. Aside from their tails, the animals have also been completely outlined and extended, and their legs are extension of the bodies with no line separations. Figs. 233-235 are examples by ancient artists whose form solutions are similar.

HORIZONTAL-VERTICAL IMAGES OF PEOPLE

Figs. 236-237 show a child's and ancient artists' drawings of human figures. The children who created figs. 238 and 239 added horizontal lines similar to those in figs. 216 and 217 for the purpose of filling empty space or showing motion. Figs. 240-242 are historical examples of similar images. The creators of figs. 243 and 244, and perhaps fig. 239 as well, seem to be aware that the horizontal-vertical direction can be used to "bend" arms and legs. While the same structure of the arms and legs can be seen in the historical comparisons (figs. 245-247), the last drawing in this group shows a transition to the next stage of line direction—variability, with acute and obtuse angles of line junctions—where the arm and leg lines meet the trunk, in the bends of the limbs, and in the feet. The hands retain the horizontal-vertical form.

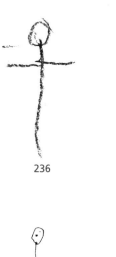

236

237

238

239

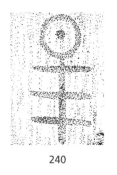

240

241

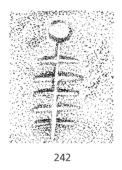

242

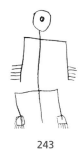

243

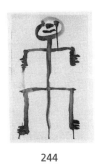

244

245

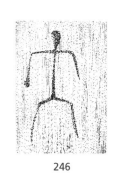

246

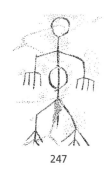

247

248

249

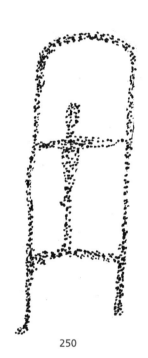

250

In "Herbert, My Brother, in Bed" (fig. 248), we see the same bent arms and legs as in the preceding figures, but with something added. The figure is organized as a perfectly structured horizontal-vertical artistic form. There is feeling for line direction only in the image of the reclining boy, while the bed is extended as an outlined rectangle. The body lies surrounded by the edges of the bed, which is the horizontal-vertical space in which it fits. The legs of the bed extend horizontally, because the child doesn't understand that they all run in one direction. Instead, he or she pictures one leg on the upper left side, another on the upper right, a leg on the lower left, and so on. (Two corresponding historical examples, figs. 249 and 250, are shown for comparison.) Young children don't say, for example, "My family and the family next door went for a walk." Instead, they say, "Mama, Daddy, Betty, Rover, Mrs. Smith, Mr. Smith, and Jane went for a walk." They think and visualize of separate and independent individuals. The abstract idea "family" as yet has no meaning, or at least no meaning that they can easily apply. Their world is created out of their own minds, and one of our tasks is to understand the underlying formative visual lawfulness according to which their minds operate.

Figs. 251 and 252, and earlier in fig. 225, we see open images with only partial outlines. Again, these children thought only in terms of line, not thickness. (Figs. 253-255 show similar forms from fourth century Egypt, sixth century France, and prehistoric Australia.)

Fig. 256 was done by a child in nursery school. When Adele drew "A Man in His House" (fig. 257), she made the man first, with an extended horizontal-vertical rectangle for the trunk of his body to which she attached the symbol for the sex organ. (Many children naturally indicate sex organs, which frequently appear in the art of primitive tribes as well; this is not unusual.) Around the man she placed a rectangular shape, open at the bottom, which she called "house." The historical comparisons in figs. 258 and 259 are almost identical.

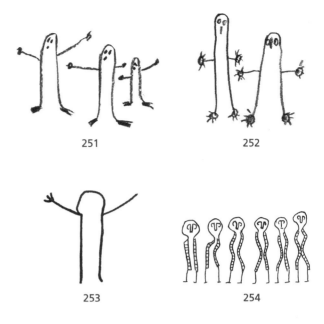

251   252

253   254

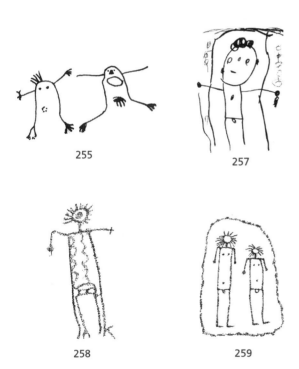

255   257

258   259

256

260

261

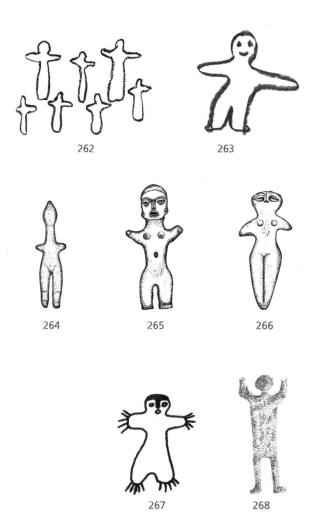

262

263

264

265

266

267

268

In "My School, My Teacher, Many Kids, and Trees in Front of the School" (fig. 260), Annette created a beautiful, organized drawing on the horizontal-vertical level. Each figure stands for itself—there are no overlapping images or figures—and all of the preceding stages are exemplified in this one drawing. Yet this is a transition stage. Although the children's bodies show width, the tree limbs and most of the children's arms are mainly linear. Annette also reverted to an earlier stage, the circle with radiating lines, in order to visualize better images of hands. (Note 7) Fred made a perfectly unified horizontal-vertical-stage drawing (fig. 261) that demonstrates his awareness of width in all its parts. The tree trunk and branches are extended as outlined elongated rectangular images, the leaves or fruit are circular, and the fruit in the baskets is circular. Each image is separated from the others by the empty paper, which, in Gestalt terms, acts as a ground that clearly, sets off all the images with figural meaning.

269

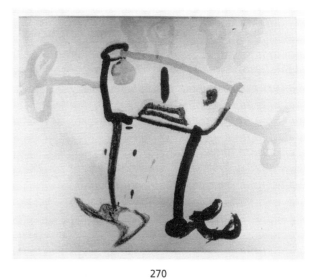

270

The drawing in fig. 262 was done by Sophie, who was able to see each figure as an entirety and completely extended and directed (outlined) them. Like this drawing, Eddy's (fig. 263) is at the horizontal-vertical stage, but Eddy had such a clear artistic conception that he drew the entire figure with a bold outline in one stroke. Historical figs. 264-268 also show an entire outline, although the first three are reproductions of sculptures and don't compare as well to Eddy's drawing as do the two-dimensional historical images, especially fig. 267. Daniel, who created "Children in the School Yard" (fig. 269), thought of each child as a whole and later added clothing and accessories. His drawing is typical of those produced by the average child who has followed his or her inner conceptions with their artistic gestalt forms. On the other hand, fig. 270 is a rare example of total visualization, with its limbs and rectangular head, at the horizontal-vertical stage of line direction. The almost round head in fig. 271, drawn by a four-year-old, is repeated in figs. 272 and 273, from ancient Peru and Persia. All three of these images also show straight noses attached to the upper portion of the circles at the greatest contrast of direction.

271

272

273

SUMMARY

We have seen numerous examples of children's art; ancient, aboriginal, or primitive art; and folk art that demonstrate the horizontal-vertical line relationship in drawings of trees and flowers, animals and people. At first, children discover this relationship and draw straight lines that meet and cross the outlines of their circular forms. Radiating lines appear around these circular shapes in a greatest contrast of direction. This is the beginning of horizontal-vertical line relationships. Then they begin to apply these lines and angles to the extremities of their images. This leads them to use the horizontal-vertical line relationship throughout most of an image. When this takes place, they have reached the full horizontal-vertical stage of line relationships in visual art. Most children between the ages of five and eight are at this developmental stage, and there are examples of work done by ancient and modern adults and older, developmentally disabled children that are at this level as well.

As older children's drawings evolve, the abrupt right angles give way to line relationships with more obtuse and acute angles. In the following chapter we will examine this new stage, the variability of line direction.

CHAPTER THREE

Variable Line Direction: Trees

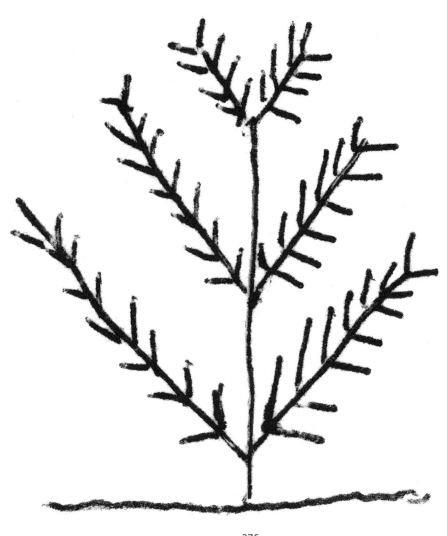

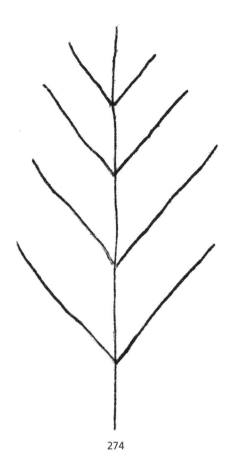

274

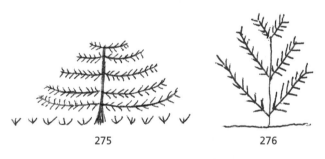

275   276

277

Children usually produce human figures and faces before they draw trees and plants, but because it is easier to see variable line direction in their drawings of the latter, we will begin there and move to drawings of people in the next chapter.

As children's experimentation continues, a new angle appears: the strict horizontal-vertical contrast gives way to more subtle relationships. Some children move into this stage between the ages of six and eight, but it is more typical of children nine years and older. In fig. 274, the parallel lines of the branches are attached to the central vertical line of the tree trunk in an example of this new stage—variable line direction. Some surmise that this new relationship comes into being simply because children see the tree, for example, in nature. But it seems more likely that children simply feel a need for change in the way they draw trees and other images. The monotony of repeating horizontal lines and angles may block them or they may respond to an intuitive urge, an archetypal experience, that grows out of their horizontal-vertical conceptions. Sharp contrasts are no longer interesting, and they move toward subtler relationships within their artistic forms. (Note 8)

Before children become fully secure in this new relationship, however, they often go through a transition stage, combining horizontal-vertical and variable line directions in one drawing (fig. 275). The trunk and large branches are horizontal-vertical, and the new angle is used only in the smaller branches. Fig. 277 shows how one child drew branches in both a horizontal-vertical direction and with variable line directions; in contrast,

278

279

280

281

282

variable line direction appears throughout the tree in fig. 276. Figs. 278-282 are historical examples of the same configuration. In fig. 283, the child confidently covered the whole page with trees and plants—all drawn in variable line directions. The children's trees in figs. 284-287 are all very similar, although the branches grow upward or downward and may be delicate or bold. Figs. 288-291 show historical comparisons from different historical periods in China, India, and Egypt. The group of floral and plant designs from prehistoric Egypt (fig. 290) further emphasizes the universality of the visual gestalt conception process.

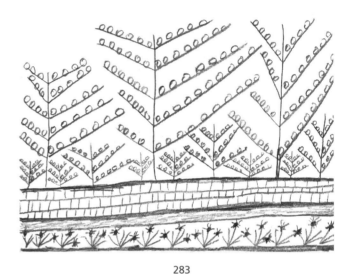

283

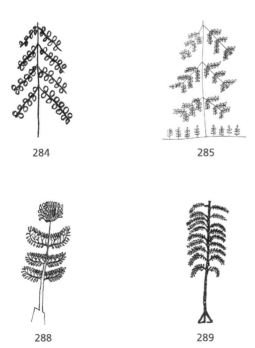

284

285

286

287

288

289

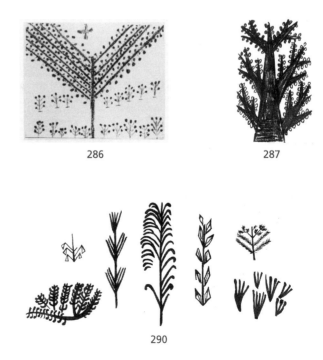

290

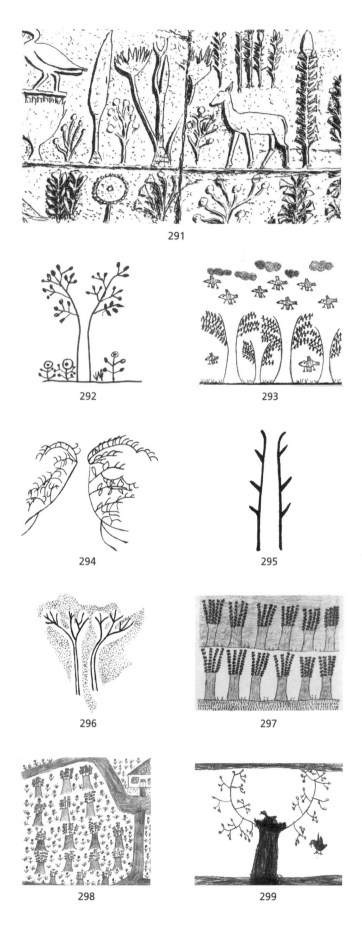

291

292

293

294

295

296

297

298

299

From the Temple of Karnak, a remarkable relief carving of the gardens of Thutmose III (fig. 291) shows exotic plants and trees that were brought to Egypt from conquered lands. This ancient artist thought in terms of single figure-ground relationships: each image stands by itself against a common empty background. The trees or plants in the upper right square show variable line direction in a simple form. Except for the circular image in the lower left section, which is a reversion, the entire relief is at the stage of variable line direction.

The child who drew the tree in fig. 292 realized that it had two edges, or borders, but wasn't yet aware of thickness or volume. He thought, "There is one side of the tree, which I can draw with a line, and there is the other side, which I can draw with a line, too." Figs. 293 and 294 are variations of this idea; figs. 295 and 296 are historical comparisons.

The tree trunks in figs. 297 and 298, however, have volume, and in both drawings the branches are expressed by lines that appear to radiate from the tops of the trunks. The plants that fill the empty spaces in fig. 298 show a similar angle. In fig. 299 an eight-year-old girl solved the intricacy of leaves and branches. When asked by her teacher why she had drawn a tree in this way, the girl thought for a moment and answered, "The tree is so big that I cannot see the top, and so I cut it off." The question forced her out of the realm of visual conception and into the territory of calculation and rationalization for an answer that would please her teacher. The world of art is a world of intuitive, organized visual structures (gestalt formations), not a world of verbalized concepts and explanations.

300

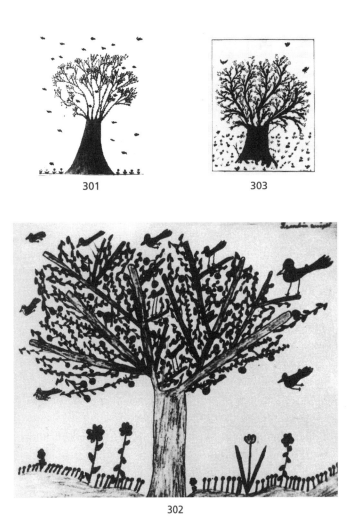

301

303

302

Four 10-year-old children produced the drawings in figs. 300-303 during a research experiment. At the time the drawings were made, the children walked by some plum trees in full bloom on their way to school every day. The suggested assignment, for those who wished to do so, was to make a drawing of a plum tree. Fifteen out of 30 children participated. Rhoda's drawing (fig. 300) shows a particular curvy quality in the branches, which are joined at an angle that she used repeatedly throughout the tree structure. May Ling drew a heavy trunk (fig. 301) that sprouted delicate wavy branches. She was at the same developmental stage, but her line and volume qualities are entirely different from the other children's. Barbara first made a thin line drawing in pencil and then grabbed a brush and painted her picture in a most powerful manner (fig. 303). Each of the girls followed her own sense of artistic form, as did Frankie, with strong angular drawing (fig. 302). All of the children were at the stage of variable line direction, but each expressed himself or herself uniquely. Figs. 304-307 are historical examples of variable line direction in tree images from various places and periods.

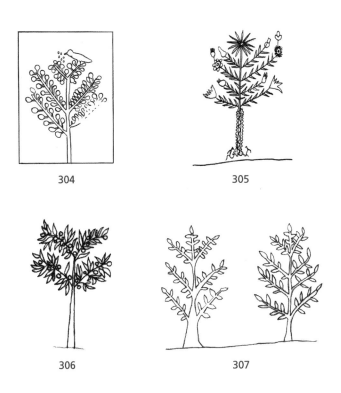

304

305

306

307

308

Children will explore the general aspects of trees and plants, painting and drawing them in innumerable ways, until they are ready to move from the general idea of "tree" to concern for a particular kind of tree (fig. 308). General characteristics are left behind, and a new outlook is experienced and recreated according to each child's abilities. Figs. 309-314 are further historical examples of individualized work at the stage of variable line direction.

309

310

311

312

313

314

315

316

317

REVERSIONS

Reversion occurs when an image is so complex that it surpasses the artist's visual grasp, and he or she must return to memories of a preceding structure or form at a stage that has been mastered. In figs. 315-317, the children held the details of their drawings together by reverting to the general conception of the circular figure in order to create a clear figure-ground relationship and, in a sense, to hold the branches and foliage together. Figs. 318-321 illustrate the historical use of this configuration.

SUMMARY

Variable line direction represents a new stage of artistic development that satisfies a need for more subtle contrasts of line direction and an interest in acute and obtuse angles. We have seen the transition from the horizontal-vertical stage to the full expression of variable line direction in contemporary and ancient drawings and paintings of trees. Examples in the next chapter will expand on this stage as it is expressed when the subjects are people and animals.

318

319

320

321

CHAPTER FOUR

Variable Line Direction: The Human Figure

322

Now let us see how variable line direction is applied to drawing the human figure. It is difficult to know if fig. 322 is an example of reversion or transition: the arms are horizontal-vertical, but the sharp angles of the legs show an inclination for variable line direction. Both the arms and legs in the next two drawings (figs. 323 and 324) indicate consciousness of variable line direction. In fig. 325, although the dresses show a new angle, the horizontal-vertical relationship remains dominant. Figs. 326 and 327 are historical counterparts of Fig. 322; figs. 328-330 are closely related to 323 and 324.

323

324

325

326

327

328

329

330

While fig. 331 is a good example of early variable line direction, it also illustrates a phenomenon that has been named the "x-ray picture," or "transparency," by some researchers. These labels imply an incorrect understanding of children's conceptions. After this child drew the legs, she felt the need to put pants over them. It was clear to her that legs are covered by trousers and not vice versa, and she saw no need to erase the lines of the legs beneath the pants. In the following illustration (332), Johnny solved his drawing in the same way: both the legs and arms are visible beneath the pants and sleeves. (He reverted to an earlier stage when he drew the hands with radiating lines.)

Fig. 333 is a transitional drawing of a group of girls whose arms show variable line direction. Each part of the body is shown clearly in the advanced drawing in fig. 334, and this child understands how sharper angles (bent limbs) can show action. Paul's drawing of a skater (fig. 335) is essentially the same as the drawings that precede and follow it (334 and 336), although one

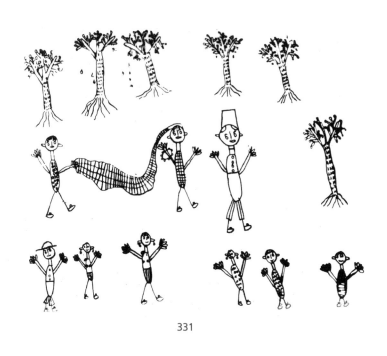

331

332

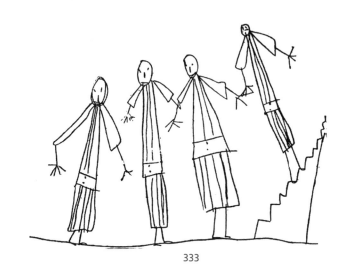

333

334

335

arm differs slightly from the other, and the angle formed by the legs also differs somewhat. Still, a new variable angle is created.

The drawing of a girl standing between two trees (Fig. 336) is particularly sensitive and interesting. Although her body covers a small area of the trees, the artist still thought in terms of simple figure-ground relationships with no overlapping images. Notice how the undulating movement in the human figure is carried throughout the picture. Both the plants and the tree branches have the same rhythm. Notice also the angle of the legs and the relationship of the head and legs to the trunk: the latter is drawn from a nearly full front perspective, but the head and legs are in profile. Some believe that such a drawing shows a confused viewpoint, but it simply expresses the artist's clearest conception. (In ancient Egyptian art, this way of depicting humans became a stylized direction that blocked natural evolutionary development for centuries.)

An expressive drawing (fig. 337) shows variable line direction in the figures of two dancers, and it is interesting that the 12-year-old artist

336

337

339

340

341

338

342

343

344

employed the technique somewhat differently in each figure. In one dancer, both arms are raised and bent, while in the other, one arm is lowered and forward though bent. The basketball player (fig. 338), drawn by another child of the same age and at the same developmental stage, is similar, but use of the left arm as a ground for the head is an interesting feature. Figs. 339-343 are historic and prehistoric examples of the same stage of development.

Fig. 344 is a reproduction of a tomb painting by an Etruscan artist, ca. 470 B.C. Variable line direction is obvious in the angles of the legs, arms, and trees, although in the tree trunks and branches we see that he reverted to a simplified structure. The harmony of movement and simplicity of line in this drawing of the original painting catch something of the joy in life that characterizes Etruscan tomb paintings.

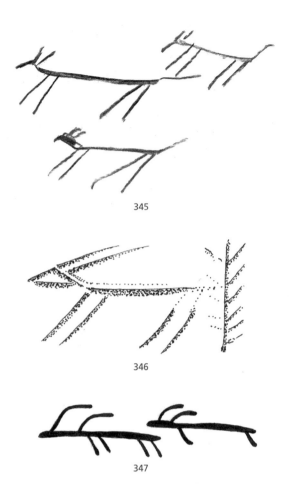

345

346

347

The stage of variable line direction is sometimes observed in the art of very young children (fig. 345). While the five-year-old was unaware of objects' width or volume, she caught the motion of a running animal by using this particular angle attached to the horizontal line indicating the body. She didn't think of each horse having four legs but instead thought of each leg alone in relation to the body. Omitting everything that wasn't important to her, she was concerned only with line relationships. (Figs. 346 and 347 are historical examples.)

While still at the early horizontal-vertical stage, another child discovered a new angle for the legs (fig. 348). He too thought in single relationships: the heads and bodies are separate outlined figures. Although the heads and torsos of each animal in fig. 349 are drawn as a unit, the legs again are considered singly and suggest a new angle. Historical examples (figs. 350 and 351) from northern Italy and Japan (1000-500 B.C.)

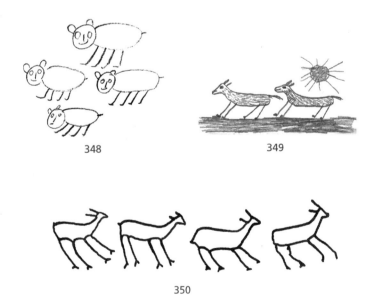

348   349

350

351

are closely related, and figs. 352-354, by artists of different ages, periods, and cultures, show how similarly each drew the legs on his or her animals. (Also see figs. 355 and 356)

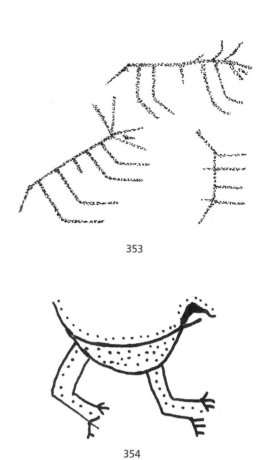

353

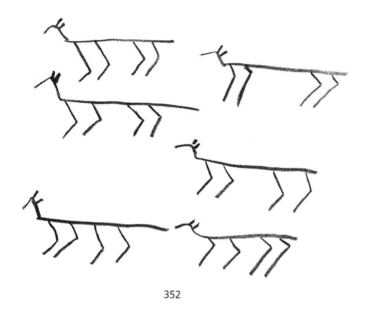

352

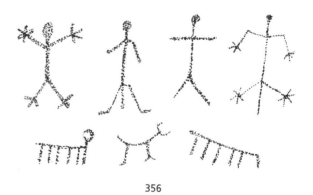

354

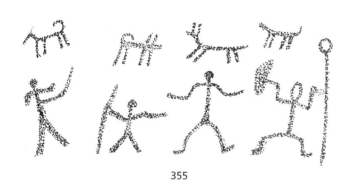

355

356

357

358

The excellent brush drawing in fig. 357 was done by an eight-year-old who applied his fine understanding of variable line direction in the animal, the trees, and the small plants. In fig. 357 we see plants scattered across the picture in an orderly fashion in order to fill the empty ground area. (Figs. 359 and 360 are historical examples of variable line direction that also indicate thickness or volume.)

In his drawing (fig. 361), Peter showed his awareness that an animal's front and back legs differ in direction relative to its body. Feeling that the space around the figures was too empty, he filled in the ground with plants and stones. The historical examples in figs. 362 and 363 are similar in line direction but are necessarily simpler than

359   360

361

362   363

the children's drawings and paintings because they were either carved in stone or modeled in clay. The children's work in figs. 364 and 365 is closely related to an engraving from paleolithic Iberia (fig. 366) and a petroglyph from the northwestern United States (367).

Eric, a very gifted 11-year-old, saw in his mind the entire structure of the animal shown in fig. 368 and drew it without taking his crayon off the paper. The early artists whose work is shown in figs. 369-371 conceived of animals in the same way. Peter's picture (fig. 372; also see fig. 361) has a nearly identical Brazilian counterpart in fig. 373. Figs. 374-377 show similarities to the children's work that we have already seen, and the completely outlined image of the horses, as well as

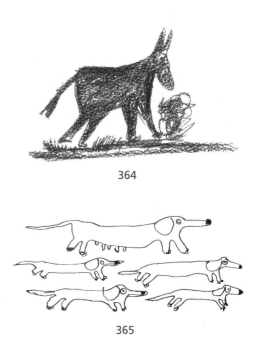

364

365

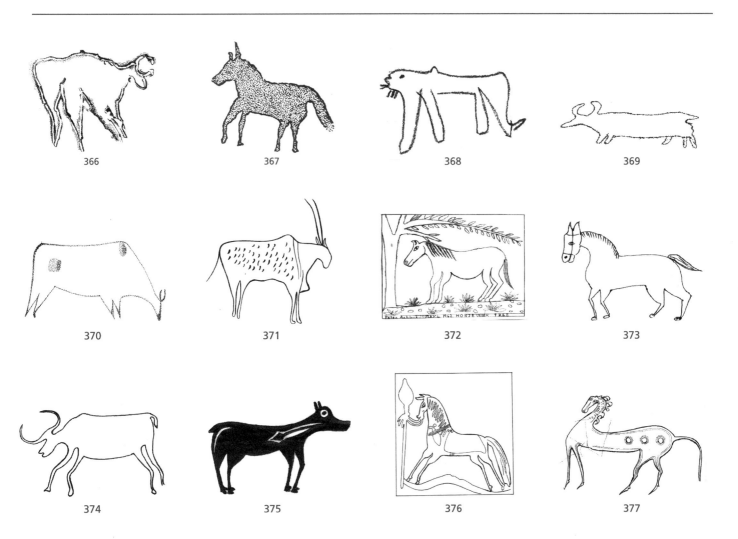

366

367

368

369

370

371

372

373

374

375

376

377

378

379

380

381

382

383

the manner in which the legs were formed, resemble each other in figs. 378 and 381. Figs. 379-383 show further examples of variability or near variability, but the riders are also of interest. Notice that both of their legs are visible in three of the drawings. From what we have learned so far, we can now understand that this does not mean they are riding sidesaddle but merely that the artists needed to show both legs.

SUMMARY

In this and the previous chapter we have compared many examples of art that illustrate the use of variable line direction. We have seen drawings of plants and trees, people and animals. Of course, children employ different line directions to draw other subjects as well, but many of these (airplanes, for example) don't lend themselves to comparison with ancient or folk art.

Variable line direction is the furthest point in the development of line and angle relationships in the artistic form. Growth continues in other areas of artistic consciousness, however, and in the next chapter we will examine figure-ground relationships.

CHAPTER FIVE

Figure-Ground Relationships

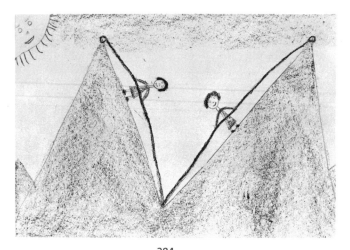

384

385

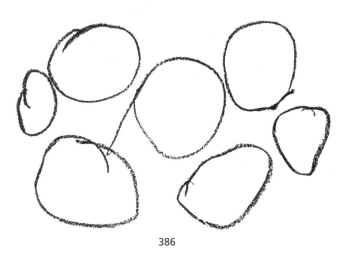

386

For many days, and even weeks, toddlers' scribbles begin on paper but continue onto the writing surface—the table or the newspaper that protects the table or perhaps the kitchen floor. But one day, as they gain greater control, they are able to contain their spiraling overlays of lines on just the paper. And there is the complete image—a "figure" against an empty "ground." Figure-ground relationships thereafter are integral to children's artistic conceptions and are basic to the existence of much of our visual art.

We define "figure" as a mark, line, or shape and "ground" as the pictorial, often empty, space that surrounds a figure and makes it visible by contrast. When a child draws or paints a landscape, he or she outlines an area near the bottom of the paper that is "earth" and another area at the top that means "sky" (fig. 384). Both are important figural areas that the child sets off clearly by a large area in the middle of the paper that becomes the empty ground. If you ask what the empty space is, you will usually be told, "It's air," but it serves to define large areas of earth and sky with the same "greatest contrast" that we have seen in children's horizontal-vertical line relationships. Although the figural images are the important aspects of an artistic conception, there is a balance between them and the ground that varies in complexity and character from one conception to another. (Note 9)

PRIMARY FIGURE-GROUND RELATIONSHIPS

In fig. 385 we see an example of a common "scribble" of continuous spiraling lines surrounded by the empty ground area. Later, as children eliminate lines and create ovals and circular images (fig. 386), each of these figures is set side by side, without overlapping, against a common empty ground. (At times, due to immature motor coordination, children's outlines may touch or cross other outlined forms, but this is accidental.) The necessary balance between figures and ground is usually created intuitively, not calculated or conceptualized. As long as the figure is simple, the problem of form can be solved simply, but when the figure becomes more complicated, the solution is likewise more difficult. The visual result of any solution communicates a wholeness, an intuitive gestalt formation.

DIFFERENTIATED GROUND AREAS

When older children, adolescents, and adults include many details in their images, many of them feel the need to differentiate ground areas as well. Figure-ground solutions can be seen in Billy's drawing, "It's Raining" (fig. 387) and in Joan's painting, "My Brother and Me" (fig. 388). With her paint-laden brush, Joan placed her two figures on the paper and then studied her picture with its empty ground for awhile. She seemed to be in a dilemma and turned around several times to see if her teacher was watching her or about to offer any comment. Then Joan carefully resumed her work. The poster paint on her brush had become a little dry by now, but without paying much attention to that, she painted with great concentration, placing spots by spots in certain places within the ground area. The result of Joan's intelligent creation, her visual thinking, was an early gestalt formation in her art.

The particular problem of artistic form that Joan solved—the figure-ground relationship—is one that all of us who engage in artistic activity experience and resolve in various ways and with various degrees of success. We wonder what was going on in Joan's mind. What psychic reasons might have underlain her actions? The strength of Joan's figures created an overwhelming contrast to the empty surroundings that she must have felt needed to be "fixed." By placing spots or marks in the empty ground surrounding the figures, which she had colored black, she solved her problem. This was not a purely external problem of picture making but one of overcoming a state of uneasiness by properly solving the figure-ground relationship. In a sense Joan's solution was intuitively realized, since it came from within her conscious-

387

388

389

390

391

392

393

ness of visual, artistic form. The basic early problem of pictorial construction that Joan solved is the fear of emptiness, or horror vacui (this is the tendency, in art, to fill all the available pictorial space with decorative or other motifs, as if "afraid of a vacuum.")

Another reason for Joan's addition of spots in the ground area may have been an attempt to anchor her main figures, to keep them from appearing to float in empty space. (This subconscious perception and solution will be addressed in chapter 6 as a reason for base lines in visual art.) It could be that children who are at Joan's stage differentiate the ground for the same reason, in addition to having some anxiety about emptiness.

A plant in a pot and "The Sea Animals (figs. 389 and 390 respectively) show how two children solved the problem of empty space in their ground areas. Deann filled her painting with the fishes' air bubbles and thereby created a compact, solid structure. The physical certainty of her artistic form, combined with her inner mental certainty, is the culmination.

The earliest relation between figure and ground is realized by using the initial forms of visual conception—the short strokes and the circular images, ovals, and angular shapes—to fill in the empty ground areas. This is seen in children's art and in some examples from early epochs (figs. 391-393).

394

395

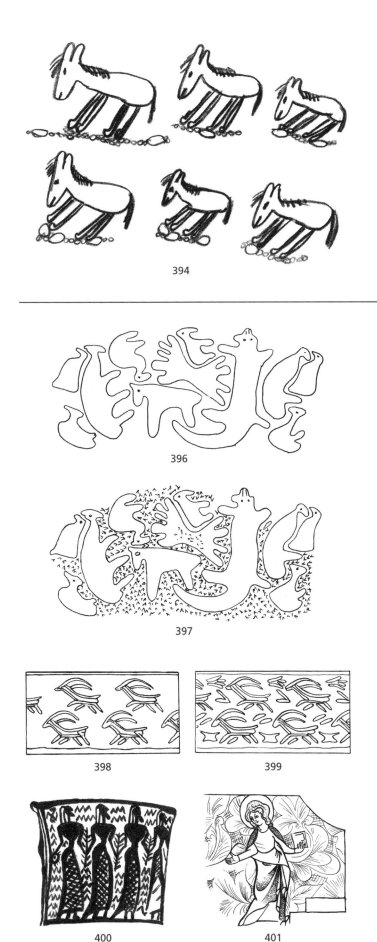

396

397

398

399

400

401

John's drawings (figs. 394 and 395) could be labeled "Problem" and Solution." In fig. 394 he depicted six horses. Their sameness—the circular body and head outlines on four legs—indicates a firmly established visual and mental attitude. In order to give the animal forms a secure position in his pictorial space, John placed a base line consisting of large and small pebbles under each one. Encouraged by his teacher to observe and evaluate his work, John remarked after a few minutes, "I know what to do. I'll make a new picture." In fig. 395 he used the same shape for the horses' bodies but drew the legs differently: the variable line directions suggest movement. In the relationship between the figures and ground, John discovered something new—a differentiated ground area. The empty ground between the horses in the first drawing is now filled with different plant shapes. These don't detract from the importance of the animals but create a close relationship between them and the ground.

In fig. 396, the author purposely omitted the markings in the ground areas to show the need for filling this space, as the artist did in the original work (fig. 397). Figs. 398 and 399 also show this type of comparison. The principle of differentiated grounds is shown in an example of an early Greek funeral pitcher (fig. 400) and in a copy of a 13th century Norwegian altar picture (fig. 401). In the figure of the saint, which stands against a ground containing large plants, we can see the light and

402

dark folds of the robe. The complex figure is set off from its differentiated ground, which is nearly as complex, yet there is a unity of form in the total figure-ground statement. A simple idea of form can yield similar results in the classroom where children's artistic formations are encouraged.

A young boy painted the clown in fig. 402 exuberantly with a large brush. Although he worked a bit carelessly, his mental image is clear. The rough diamond shapes on the coat demanded more than an empty ground so, after a moment of thought, he placed stripes of various widths, as well as some circular shapes, in the area next to the clown. When the floor seemed too empty, he filled that space with various spots of different tones. The results are crude, but his efforts produced an organized figure-ground relationship.

The following two case studies (figs. 403-406 and 407-410) demonstrate the primary figure-ground relationship in relatively complicated pictorial structures. The students chose the themes and were encouraged to work as slowly as possible and to avoid any noise and other distractions. The quiet setting and deliberate pace made it easier for them to assess their progress and results.

The theme of the first case study was "A Party Under a Big Tree" (fig. 403). Emy conceived of her picture in terms of single figure-ground relationships—each figure standing for itself without any overlapping against a common empty ground. After she placed the tree at the bottom of the paper, she organized the children's figures in an alternating boy-girl pattern. All the figures are horizontal-vertical forms. (The girls' figures are emphasized because of their black hair.) When Emy finished her picture, she was advised to look at it closely for awhile and then was asked how she liked it. She answered at once, "The big tree is too empty—I want to make the leaves dark also, like the hair of the girls." In a few minutes, after she had done this (fig. 404), she immediately decided to "make the whole tree dark." That was quickly accomplished, but it presented her with another problem. In an excited voice, Emy declared, "I have to make all the shoes dark and

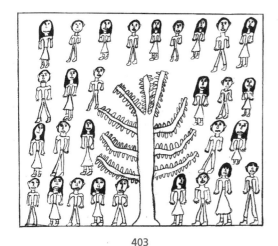

403

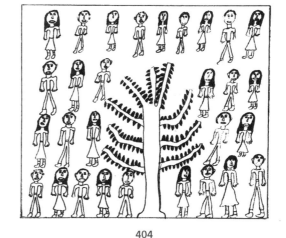

404

405

406

the sweaters of the boys dark, too" (fig. 405).

From the perspective of working out the total structure, the concern here was for the relationship of the large tree to all the small figures that served to differentiate the ground. As the picture developed, the individual figures gained stronger figural meaning within the total ground area (that is, the contrast between them and the empty, light ground was heightened).

Emy came to class the next week with a certain excitement in her voice. "I was thinking all the time about my picture," she said. "The children don't stand on anything." The teacher asked her where the party had taken place. When Emy explained that there was a pasture around the tree, the teacher said, "Why don't you show the pasture?" Emy then placed flowers and grass between the children's figures. With that she attained a solid hold in the pictorial space of the ground (fig. 405).

Emy expressed great surprise, and concern, when she declared, "Now there are empty spaces between the children! The spaces are too open." Her judgment was correct; she saw the figure-ground of the large dark tree in relation to the remainder of the highly differentiated ground. With the greatest care and concentration, she filled in the rest of the open ground with flowers and plants. Now she had obtained an effect in which the main figure, the tree, stood out clearly from a highly differentiated ground (fig. 406). The same effect can be seen in the relation between the children and the plants. The whole picture, constructed on the basis of a unified figure-ground relationship, now gives an effect that is similar to Oriental miniatures, painted or woven wall hangings, European rugs of the Middle Ages (Late Period), and folk art from various times.

CONSCIOUSNESS OF ARTISTIC FORM

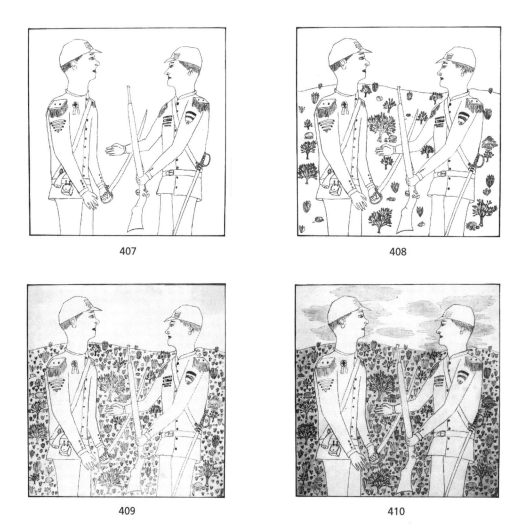

407

408

409

410

The theme of the second case history stemmed from a boy's interest in the Civil War. In the first version of his picture (fig. 407), he drew two soldiers, the one on the left surrendering to the other. It was never necessary to remind this student to concentrate: by nature he was a slow and careful draftsman, and the posture of both soldiers is an indication of his visual conception of totality of form. Soon he realized that his figures needed a background: "They have to be somewhere," he said. For a landscape he drew a hill dotted with trees and bushes, rocks and flowers (fig. 408). Reminded that he should take some time to evaluate his picture, he exclaimed, "It's hard to see which is which. I'll make the background darker and put in more grass, rocks, and

flowers." Still, Kenneth was not completely satisfied, for he discovered that the solders' heads also needed emphasis. "They need a darker background, but not too dark," he observed (fig. 409).

But when he saw the picture again a week later, he wasn't satisfied. "The soldiers are too close to the background. It has to be much darker," he decided. When he added even more small objects to the ground area and darkened them, he brought the soldiers and the ground into a balanced relationship or a total gestalt formation (fig. 410). Finally, the total solution of the figure-ground relationships resulted here, as in the previous example, in a self-sustained whole that gives the picture its artistic quality.*

*Both Emy and the boy who made the Civil War drawings were guided by the author's questions to observe their work, compare parts, determine what they liked and what bothered them, and pose possible solutions in order to make their work more acceptable to them, or "better," according to their own standards.

A stone relief from the 9th century was conceived in the same way (fig. 411). In fig. 412 the placement of the figures in a Peruvian tapestry is similar, but the weaver placed small angular shapes between the main figures. There is very little ground in fig. 413 because the characters nearly touch one another, but texture in the ground area of fig. 414 sets off the engraved figures.

Sometimes there is no need for ground differentiation. In a hospital scene (fig. 415), Paula placed beds, people, and bedside tables one above the other to fill the entire page. Another girl made her two horses entirely visible by placing one above the other on a powerful ground of black paper (fig. 416). From about 2000-1700 B.C., we see horses pulling a wagon or chariot as depicted on a cylindrical seal. No differentiation is needed in the ground area as the figures encompass the entire space (fig 417).

411

412

413

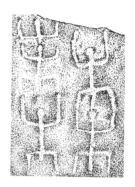
414

415

416

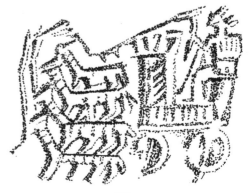
417

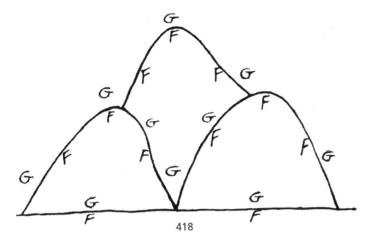

418

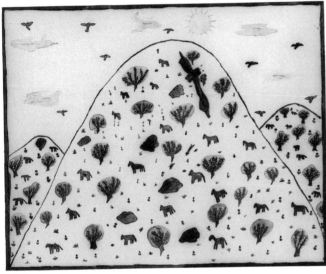

419

THE BORDERLESS TRANSITION FROM FIGURE TO GROUND

From closely juxtaposed to overlapped figures seems a small step, and yet it is significant. Not until children are around nine years old do they begin to deliberately overlap large figures in their drawings and paintings with smaller ones or overlap large figures—hills or mountains—with each other. The earth and sky are no longer treated as separate figures placed above and below an intervening empty space. In older children's art, the sky is extended downward to touch the upper borderline of the earth figure. Now its meaning shifts in a gradual manner that lacks any borders* from figure to ground, from sky to background. This occurs first in overlapped, outlined images with no graduated shading and later in overlapped images with graduated shading.

The use of primary figure-ground relationships for smaller subjects, such as people and animals, and overlapping large figures, such as hills, usually continues for quite some time.

OVERLAPPING OUTLINED FIGURES WITHOUT SHADING

In the diagram of three hills in an overlapping group (fig. 418), F signifies "figure," and G signifies "ground." The inner areas of the two front hills, near and along their outlines, have figural meaning all the way to the base line, and the middle hill has figural meaning in the area just inside its outline between the points where the outline touches each adjacent hill. These figural meanings shift gradually and "borderlessly" into ground meanings in the two front hills near their bases and in the middle hill all along the areas near the outlines of its neighboring hills. The ground areas of the middle hill serve as background for the hills in front of it. The earth has figural meaning in the area below and along the base line of the hills, or upper borderline of the

*"Borderless" means that the figural meaning within an image of an overlapping group of images changes gradually to ground meaning with no border line separating the two meanings.

earth figure. The following examples should make this clear. David painted a hill that overlaps smaller hills on each side (fig. 419). The ground meaning of the smaller hills sets off the central hill, and small figures of horses, flowers, rocks, and trees are placed in close juxtaposition here and there across the hills in primary figure-ground relationships. This is a very good example of a transition stage in David's visual conception.

That is, details of the objects on each hill do not overlap one another and therefore represent the primary stage of figure-ground relationships.

In fig. 420 we see how Stuart drew many overlapping hills with people, trees, goats, and pathways (plus a lookout house near the top of the picture). Again, areas within the outlines of each mountain have figural meaning, but areas that are next to the outlines of the mountains overlapping them have ground meaning. The small figures are placed in a primary figure-ground relationship against an empty ground within each mountain. The hills overlap the sky in both figures, and the ground meaning of the areas of sky near the hills sets them off.

Fred painted only one large mountain against the sky (fig. 421), which has a much smaller figural area because it serves as ground for clouds and birds. The mountain is almost entirely covered with trees, which overlap each other and the mountain. Each tree is outlined. This reversion to the circular and oval image stage allowed Fred to contain the detailed branches and overlap them without visual confusion. Again, the area of each tree that is near the overlapping outline of another tree has ground meaning. Such figural and ground contrasts are fundamental to visual art. In contrast, camouflage is so effective because it seeks to duplicate "ground" only, eliminating the differences in color, texture, etc. that normally allow us to distinguish "figure" from the surroundings.

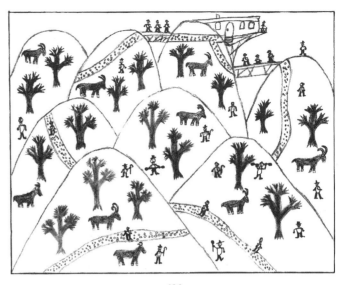

420

421

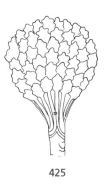

422 423 424 425

426

427 428

429

The overlapping hills in figs. 422 and 423 are 11th century examples. The bushes and trees don't overlap, as they do in Fred's painting, but are placed in primary figure-ground relationships as in David's and Stuart's works. Figs. 424 and 425, historical examples from India and Poland, show overlapping foliage.

Multiple overlappings of small figures are seen in another drawing by Stuart (fig. 426). Note that he omitted the lower legs and feet from his figures behind the first row; we will return to this point later in the chapter. His arrangement of the figures—five in front and then rows of four and three behind that—is interesting, but we do not know his intent. Was it to allow space for the street light and bus sign, or were those merely afterthoughts?

The historical examples in figs. 427 and 428 illustrate the same practices, but the saints' halos in the latter drawing are of interest. Each serves as an empty ground area to set off the head of an important person so that, in a group, that person attains prominence. The halo therefore has both visual and symbolic significance. In fig. 429, the human heads are overlapped in such a way that those in back have scarcely any meaning. When overlapping causes key features of an image to be hidden in this way, confusion can result.

430

431

In contrast, Dorianne's fine drawing (fig. 430) was done with the utmost clarity and is far beyond the visual expressions of many high school and college students who try to reproduce images of live models in a piecemeal manner from a set viewpoint. Constant copying often locks young minds and attitudes into a rigid system of perception and expression. Artists need to go within themselves and find their own honest ways of seeing the world around them. Dorianne could do that with a little guidance that led her to evaluate and improve upon her conceptions.

Paul showed the same artistic consciousness when he created "Women Waiting for the Opening of a Food Store" (fig. 431). The "textures" of the women's dresses help set off one figure from another. (Figs. 432 and 433 show similar overlappings in historical artworks.)

432

433

434

435

436

437

"Two Hippies" (fig. 434) shows a woman's head overlapping a man's, and his long hair serves as a contrasting ground for her light profile. Helen's drawing, more delicately rendered (fig. 435), is otherwise similar, as are examples from ancient Egypt and Greece (figs. 436 and 437). The textures of the middle and right heads in the Egyptian picture create nice contrasting ground areas for the overlapping profiles.

Overlapping objects requires some artistic form organization, but overlapping figures of animals with four long legs is an altogether different challenge. In fig. 438, Albert drew wild horses running. His placement of alternating light and dark horses makes each horse visible, and he didn't attempt to show the front legs and hooves of the horses behind the front one. To have done so would have been visually confusing as well as unnecessary. Beverly's "Wild Horse Stampede" (fig. 439) isn't as successful, because she wanted to include all the legs.

438

439

440

441

In a different medium (fig. 440), a boy carved a mare and her colt in plaster of paris. The colt is clearly indicated as a figure against the ground area of the stone wall, the sky, and its mother's body. Heidi drew two well-organized horses (fig. 441): the front horse's head and neck overlap the darker horse's body in just the right way to create a clearly conceived artistic form. The ground areas between the horses' legs are sufficiently wide to set each leg off well, also.

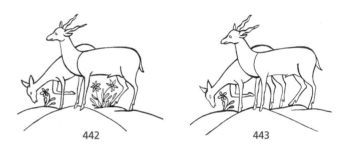

442   443

Figs. 442 and 443 show two drawings based on an original Persian painting. In the second figure, all of the legs have been added. In the original conception, however, the artist wisely omitted the deer's legs and painted flowers in their place. Debbie's sculptural relief (fig. 444) also shows overlappings that are artistically solved: only the body of the front dog and all of the dogs' necks and forelegs can be seen. Although the hind legs of one dog are not shown at all, the sculpture feels complete and displays an artistic wholeness. This solution to the problem of visual confusion is seen time and again in historical and folk art. The historical comparison (fig. 445) shows the same elimination of legs in order to achieve an artistic gestalt formation with overlapped figures.

444

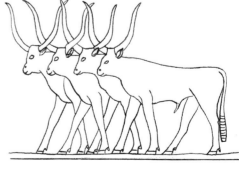

445

446

In fig. 446, a complex outline drawing, the girl's figure is set off by the ground provided by the chair and wallpaper. The texture of the sweater and the hair, as well as the pattern of the skirt, required that the artist bring a pattern into the wall ground for balance. In Dieter's "Bird on a Branch of a Cherry Tree" (fig. 447), the veins in the overlapping feathers and leaves create textural patterns. Although there is no shading, he drew the lines on the background leaves closer together to create a darker value and thus greater visual clarity throughout the leaves.

447

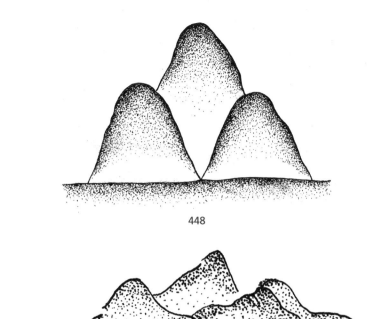

448

449

BORDERLESS TRANSITIONS WITH SHADED FIGURAL AND GROUND MEANINGS

The author shaded each figural area in fig. 448 to make the reality of the borderless transition more apparent. As the shading gradually lessens in value the figural meaning becomes ground meaning with no shading. The clear contrast between figural and ground areas is also seen in historical art (figs. 449-451) and in Kenneth's drawing (fig. 452).

Figural meanings are shaded in "Goats in Hills" (fig. 453) as well, but this wonderful drawing is also an outstanding example of clearly developed artistic vision. People who saw this and Debby's other works (e.g., fig. 454) couldn't believe that she had produced these images from her own head. Note that in addition to shaded figural meanings in the hawk drawing, there are shaded ground areas. Susan used the shading of figural meaning to overlap three bushes and earth mounds (fig. 455).

450

451

452

453

454

455

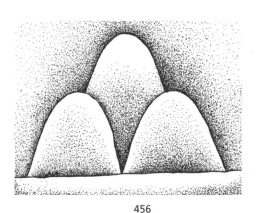

456

457

458

459

460

In fig. 456, the author drew three overlapping mountains, shading the ground areas. The dark sky around the mountains shows up their light figural areas, and the earth, also light, is visible only because it contrasts with the dark mountain bases. The outlines dissolve into the dark ground areas and really are no longer needed. Figs. 457 and 458 are examples of historical paintings with shaded ground.

In the work of Debby and Susan (figs. 454 and 455), we saw shading in both the figural and ground areas. Judd's ink and water picture of a mountain (fig. 459) includes figures with shading and ground that is lightly shaded, unshaded, and shaded. One-sided shading of figural areas sometimes appears in old maps, and it is also seen here in an ancient Roman wall painting (fig. 460). The foreground rock formation is set off by a light ground area outside, by its shaded contour, and by a shaded ground area around the shaded left side. (Also see figs. 461 and 462.)

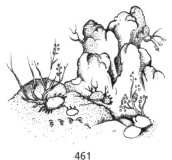

461

462

463

464

465

466

The variable use of shading occurs also in drawings and paintings of the human face and head, as in fig. 463. The hair and the nostril (figural areas) and the neck near the jaw (ground) are shaded. The light eyelids are set off by a shaded ground area. Frederick retained some outlining for the forehead, nose, and chin. In Debby's self-portrait (fig. 464), the end of the nose is shaded, and the sides and nostrils are set off by the light ground area of the cheek. The hair is shaded, and textures along the left side of the face make it more visible. The ground area of the neck is shaded, while the figure of the chin is light. Yet, to the right, the edge of the jaw is a shaded figure against the light ground of the neck. The nose is a light figure set off by shading on both sides, and the corners of the eyes are similarly set off by a shaded ground area.

Finally, figs. 465 and 466—both sensitive and subtle—display similar uses of shading. All of these portraits display originality and a complex artistic order and unity.

SUMMARY

This exploration of figure-ground relationships began with outlined figures set side by side against an empty ground and progressed to overlapping large figures, the borderless transition stage of the figure-ground relationship, and various combinations of shaded figural and ground areas resulting in sophisticated and complex images. We saw in the examples how the figure-ground relationship evolves as children's cognitive and evaluative abilities mature and, again, how ancient art mirrors the developmental stages we see in children's art.

In the next chapter we will look at the use of base lines in artistic space.

CHAPTER SIX

Spacial Orientation

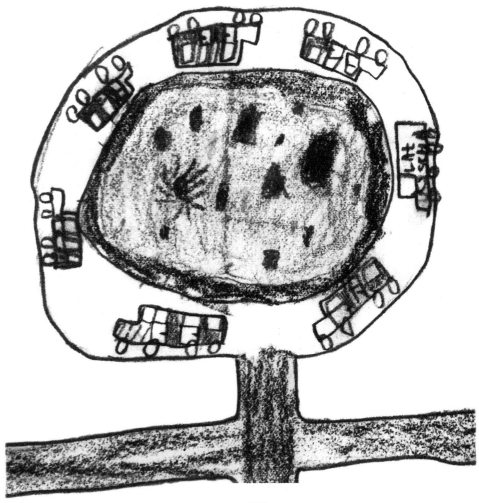

467

468

Almost as fundamental to works of visual art as figure-ground relationships, spatial relationships consist of the arrangement of images within the overall pictorial space. At best, the shape, size, color, light to dark value, location, and orientation of each image in an artwork are considered for the sake of the whole. In fact, they determine one another's nature within the entirety. Such unity of images within the overall space of a drawing, painting, etc. does not always occur, however. If the sense for artistic form has not been developed, the result may be isolated, independent images with separate and unrelated directions or clashing lines and angles, colors and values, etc. However, the sense of artistic unity, as it deals with spatial relationships, can be developed in art students, children and adults, if their teachers possess an active sense for artistic form and knowledge of how to encourage it in their students.

The placement and orientation of figures in an artistic space can have infinite variations. For the most part, though, the configurations follow stages of development, just as do line and shape and figure-ground relationships. From the isolated but similar figures placed here and there on paper by young children, there is a gradual change until figures achieve a unified direction. From the single horizontal or curved base line upon which children anchor their figures, there is a transition to multiple, individual, and implied base lines. From parallel, rectangular, and circular or oval base lines, some older children begin to place figures in such close juxtaposition that no base line is needed.

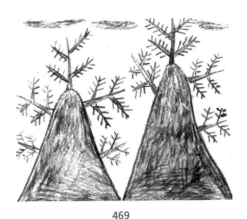

469

470

ISOLATED DIRECTION WITHOUT BASE LINES

Very young children place their figures on paper at random: they draw or paint one image and, turning their papers, create others. No base line, no sky, no top nor bottom is indicated. They did the same thing at an earlier stage when they conceived of their first circular images, and when they begin to express images that adults recognize as people or animals, they continue to use the same approach (fig. 467).

Teachers or other adults may notice that, around the age of six or seven, children begin to draw or paint a line on which they place their images. This base line has several uses, but its main purpose, we believe, is to provide stability or a visual (and mental) "hold" that prevents figures from seeming to float or shift in the space on the paper. In addition to providing a foundation, base lines also allow for orderly placement of images.

471

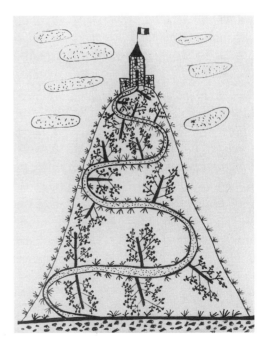

472

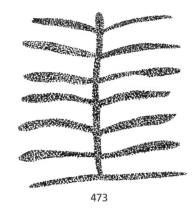

473

474

475

SINGLE OR DOUBLE BASE LINES

At first the bottom edge of the paper may serve as a base line (figs. 468-470), or a single horizontal line across the entire picture serves as both the borderline of the earth in children's early landscapes and as a base line (figs. 471 and 472). In 471, the rooftops also serve as base lines. When John made this drawing, he understood intuitively that chimneys and roofs usually have a perpendicular relationship. This understanding causes his chimneys to look tilted. At a later stage, when John understood more about unity of direction, he would no doubt place his chimneys upright in a parallel relation to the houses and trees. The mountain climbers in fig. 384 and the trees in figs. 469 and 472 have the same relationship to the mountain sides that John's chimneys do to his houses.

Fig. 470 is unusual because it contains so many base lines. It was drawn by a woman whose mental age was measured at six years and whose I.Q. was 49. Nevertheless, she had a remarkable ability to organize her drawing in a harmonious way, and she was an enthusiastic participant in a class at Southbury Training School in Connecticut. The bottom edge of her paper is the base line for the rounded hills, and the hills provide a base line for the trees or plants, which follow their curvature. Birds fly above, each with its own base line to hold it in position (see the section on individual base lines, p. 94 in this chapter). The circular disk of the sun serves as base line for the rays.

Rock engravings and paintings in figs. 473-474 show the same use of single horizontal base lines that we have seen in the children's art.

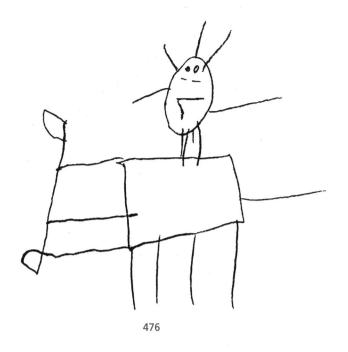

476

477

478

Fig. 471, already mentioned, is an excellent and typical example of a single full horizontal base line. The drawing in fig. 476 was done by a child who was only three and a half, an unusually early age for using base lines. He or she used part of the outline of the horse as a base line for the rider. There are two base lines in fig. 477, the upper borderline of the earth and the outline of the horse's back.

"Flight into Egypt" (fig. 478) is an unusual drawing. The donkey's back becomes the base line for Mary, whose extended arm is the base line for Jesus. Each character's fingers and hair radiate from circular or oval shapes. Although Traudl reverted to an early stage of circles with radiating lines in order to express hands and fingers, notice how precise she was when she drew exactly five fingers on each hand. Figs. 479-483 show historical examples of related subjects that were resolved in the same fashion. In "American Marines on Boat" (fig. 484), the boat deck serves as the logical base line for the marines (also see figs. 485 and 486).

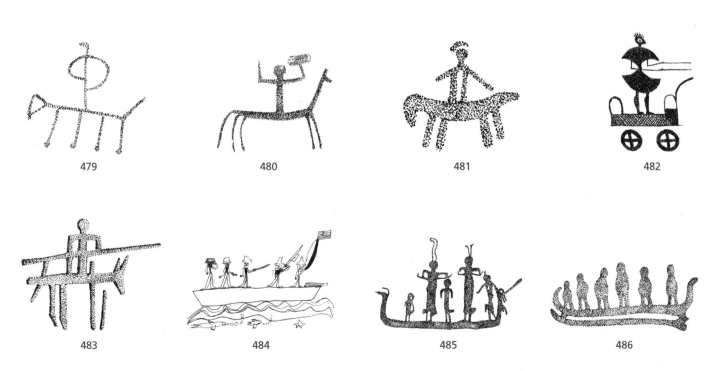

479

480

481

482

483

484

485

486

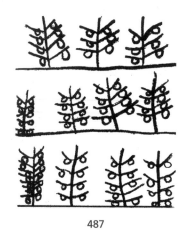

487

488

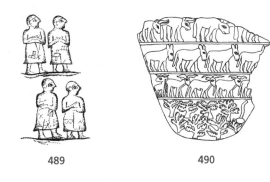

489   490

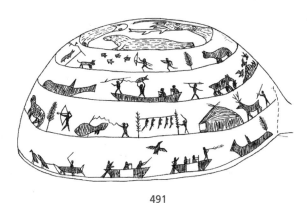

491

MULTIPLE BASE LINES

Multiple base lines provide more opportunities—more subjects can be included and "fixed" in the pictorial space. Peter and David (see figs. 487 and 488) used multiple and parallel base lines. The trees and vehicles on the upper lines are meant to be more distant, not higher. At first children will make similar figures the same size, regardless of their position relative to one another, but eventually they understand that objects farther from the viewer look smaller and draw them accordingly, still placing them higher in the picture. (See the varied uses of base lines in art from the past in figs. 489-491.)

Donald used six base lines in his "A Small Town in Connecticut" (fig. 492), and, to indicate increasing distance, he made the spaces between the lines smaller as they approached the top of the paper. To anchor his houses, he set them onto base lines, one above the other. It is easier to understand why Donald proceeded in this way if we also understand that he had not yet conceived of overlapping figures. For example, Bob drew two base lines with houses to show both sides of "Virginia Street" (fig. 493), although in doing so he obscured part of the street. (Also see fig. 524). Unbothered by this, Bob gave the houses a unified direction. Later in the chapter are solutions with buildings that do not overlap the street.

In figs. 494-496, base lines reach across the picture in some places and curve upward in others. A Bantu boy (fig. 494) kept his images from appearing to float in space in the same way as did an ancient Egyptian (fig. 495) and a modern 12-year-old, Edward (fig. 496), whose elaborate picture of a town shows streets running horizontally, vertically, and diagonally. The streets are overlapped only by a few small images of animals and people. Houses and trees are placed along the upper borders of the streets, but a few trees can be found on their own individual base lines. Some of the houses appear to have only one side and the front, and others show only the front.

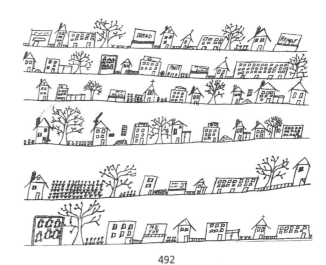

492

493

494

495

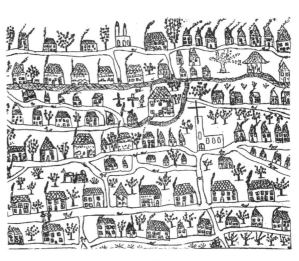

496

CONSCIOUSNESS OF ARTISTIC FORM

497

498

499

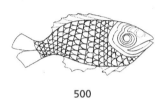

500

Occasionally, base lines occur within a figure. For example, Elizabeth, wanting to show feathers on her owl (fig. 497), discovered that she could draw half-circle or scallop-shaped feathers on base lines within the outline of the bird. Since she was at the beginning stage of figure-ground relationships, she placed each feather next to an adjacent one with no overlapping. It should be clear that these base lines, and the majority of those we have observed (figs. 476-486), are not used only to indicate motion, as some believe. Most base lines, in fact, have nothing to do with motion but instead, as we have shown, help the artist fix his or her figures in pictorial space. Eduard's feathers—and base lines (fig. 498)—are more complex than Elizabeth's but still illustrate the same principle. Similar solutions are shown in figs. 499 and 500.

VIEWPOINT

In any visual artistic conception, there is no "correct" viewpoint from which we should see or express what we perceive. Front views, side views, etc. are intellectually contrived systems for seeing only certain aspects of an object, and they are rarely expressed artistically in a holistic conception. In other words, few objects are painted or drawn solely from a single perspective.

CIRCULAR BASE LINES

We have already seen a few examples of circular or curving base lines like Richard's (fig. 501), whose circular figure becomes a base line for all of the figures standing around it. Notice how Richard reverted to the earliest horizontal-vertical line and angle relationship—the circle with radiating lines. His "Ring Around the Rosie" players are placed perpendicular to the circle's outline, and their outstretched arms form a second circle parallel to the first. Mary's drawing of an oval pool with fish and apple trees (fig. 502) is very similar, and both drawings are examples of reversion, again, to the circle with radiating lines (the players, the trees, and the leaves). Likewise, in "Lake with Fish Surrounded by Mountains" (fig. 503), dark mountains appear to radiate from the base line of the circle. Ancient examples, too, show this reversion (figs. 504-506), and figs. 507-509 show a variation: the lines are drawn from the inside of the circular base line and radiate toward the center.

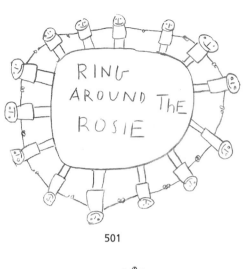

501

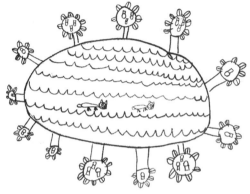

502

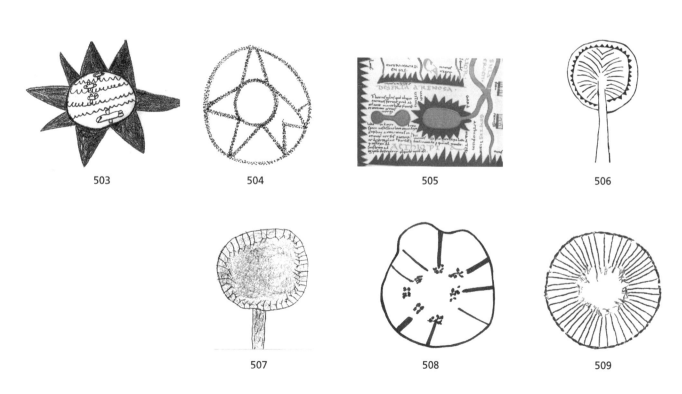

503   504   505   506

507   508   509

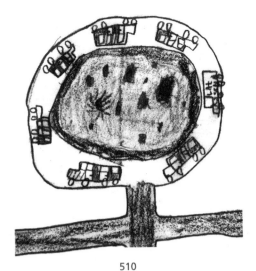

510

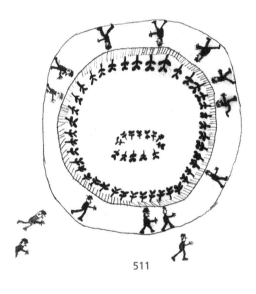

511

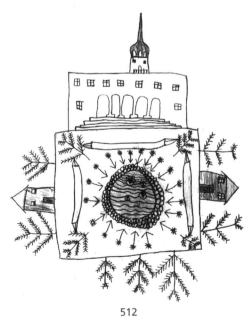

512

But of course more than simple lines have been shown to radiate from a circular form. We have seen triangular shapes (figs. 503-506) as well as ovals bisected with lines (fig. 502), and in figs. 510-515 all manner of forms radiate perpendicularly from circles. For example, Hugo (in fig. 510) placed cars and trucks in this fashion, showing them parked in a drive that encircles a park. Walter drew a circular path around a flower bed (fig. 511), placing people, grass, and flowers perpendicular to the circular forms. Note that the flowers radiate inward, as do the trees and branches of figures 507-509. Even the flowers in the small bed near the center form a near circle, although no base line was drawn for them. Eric's drawing (fig. 512) of a circular pool surrounded by stones, which serves as a base line for the flowers, is interesting because the pool and flowers are placed within a nearly square plaza that then provides four base lines for buildings and trees. (Figs. 513-515 show historical comparisons.)

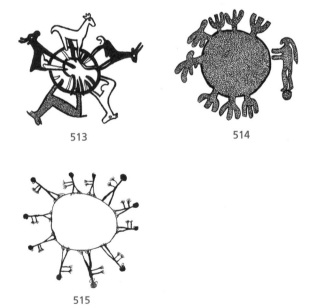

513

514

515

PARALLEL BASE LINES

During a certain stage of their artistic development, children will show a street (or river, etc.) with houses or trees, as Herman did in fig. 516. He placed a row of houses along the base lines formed by the upper borderline of the street, and when he drew the houses across the street, he drew them in the opposite direction. Both rows of houses are on base lines and yet they don't overlap the street. Because he wanted to show the street unobscured, Herman simply turned his paper around to draw the second row of houses. Compare this to fig. 493 (two rows of houses in a unified direction) and to fig. 517, a historical example from an old map.

Florence drew a stream with trees and ducks (fig. 518). Her base lines, like those in figs. 516 and 517, are parallel, and the two rows of trees are placed in opposite directions. Again, if the trees had been drawn in the same direction, the stream would have appeared blocked to Florence, and she wouldn't have been able to show the ducks or ripples of water as fully and clearly as she did. Of course, parallel lines don't need to be straight (for example, fig. 519), and when base lines change direction, so will the figures "attached" to them (figs. 520 and 521). We need to understand that there is a definite need for the kind of solution applied by these children, an old mapmaker, and ancient craftspeople.

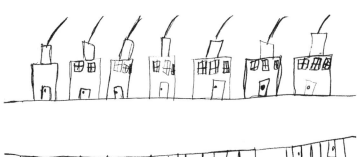

516

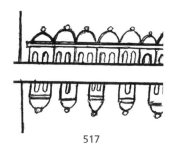

517

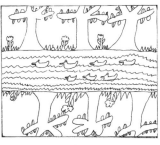

518

519

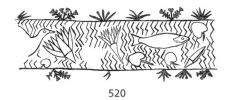

520

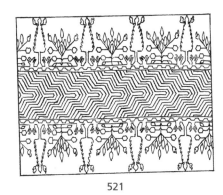

521

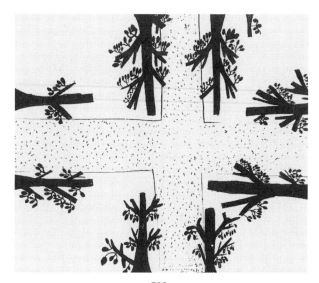

522

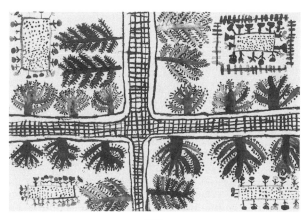

523

524

"Parkways" and "Two Roads Bordered by Trees" (figs. 522 and 523) show horizontal-vertical structures and trees with the same perpendicular relationship to their base lines. In fig. 523 this relationship is similar to those in figs. 516-518; that is, each arm of the cross formed by the two roads has parallel base lines with trees attached, and the facing rows of trees are in opposite directions. In Walter's mind, the roads are important elements that he doesn't want to obstruct, and his solution is consistent with the stage of figure-ground relationships he has attained. In fig. 522, on the other hand, a younger boy used the edges of his paper as base lines and attached his trees to the edge. Each pair of trees is parallel to the nearest part of the parkway and has a different direction than the others. The cross formations don't serve as base lines at all.

Herbert (fig. 524) drew two diagonal roads that intersect at the center of the paper and, with the exception of the lower right road, extend to each corner. The outlines of each road form parallel base lines for various images that were drawn in the same direction. The bottom edge of the paper forms another base line for trees and bushes, but there are also trees in the left triangle that were placed on base lines implied by the rows of grass. We can see, too, that all of the figures drawn along the "bottom" baseline of each road overlap the road. Chiefly, though, Herbert's drawing shows us transitions to both unified direction and implied base lines.

All of the examples in figs. 525-534 show rectangular forms with images placed along their outer edges and with each row of images in the opposite direction from the opposite row. In Elizabeth's birthday party (fig. 534), the table serves no base line function at all. Instead, she used the edge of the paper as the base line for her partygoers and allowed them to overlap the table surface.

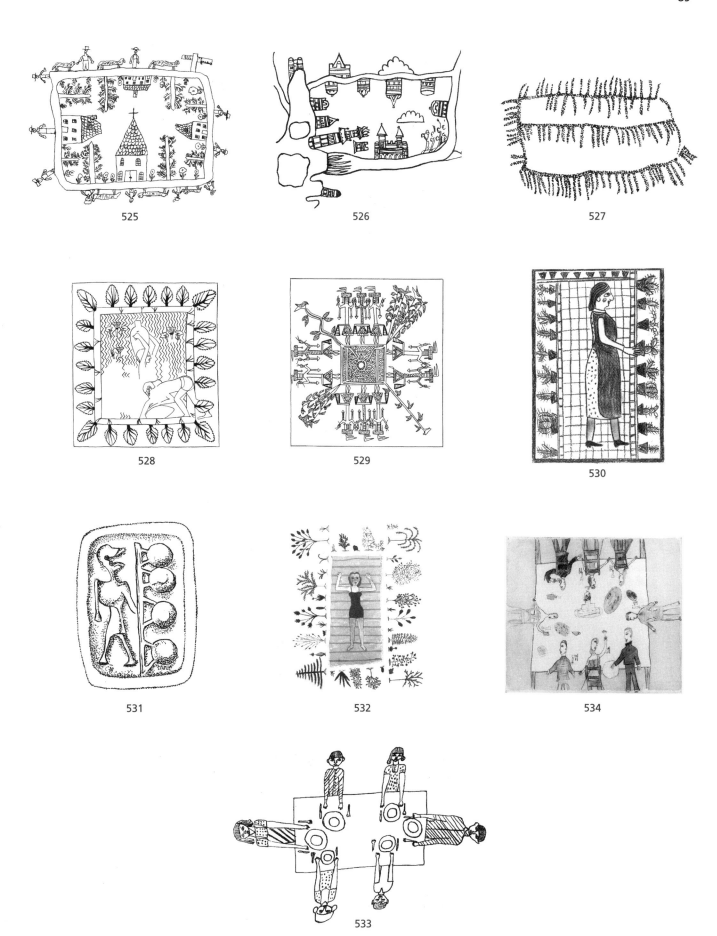

525

526

527

528

529

530

531

532

534

533

535

Not all artistic forms with similar opposed images placed in opposite directions have parallel base lines. The four dogs in fig. 535 were made by two boys. The center two are placed in opposite directions on either side of a thick base line. Eric drew two boys on a "sea saw" (fig. 536), using the cross piece as the single base line. The children's art and historical comparisons in figs. 537-542 show figures that are in opposite directions with single or parallel base lines. The wheel axles on Simone's cart (fig. 538) are attached to base lines formed by the sides of the cart. Karin's wagon has wheels on both sides (fig. 539), and her horses are placed in opposite directions on the base line that is formed by the shaft as in historic examples figs. 540-542. Other wagons or chariots, each with a team of horses or mules attached to a shaft, are shown in figs. 543-547. In this group, however, the animals have been placed in a single direction. All of the wheels are fully visible circles.

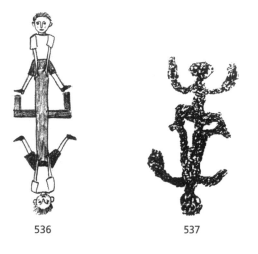

536   537

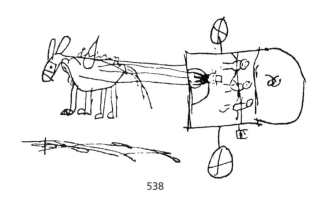

538

539

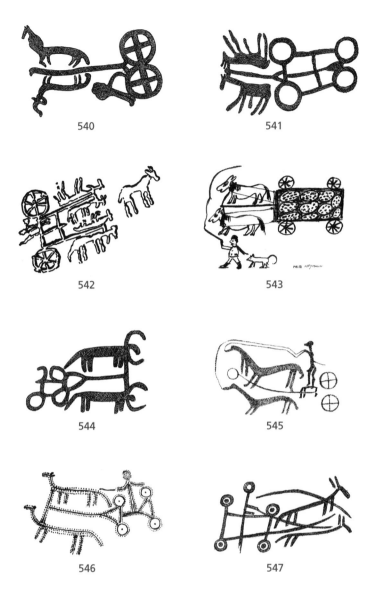

540

541

542

543

544

545

546

547

TRANSITION TO UNIFIED DIRECTION

In drawings and other works that contain many images, we often find a transition stage between opposite and unified directions. For example, in the drawing of the swimming pool (fig. 548), a row of people stands at the bottom edge of the paper and another row is on a horizontal base line formed by the upper border of the pool. Both rows stand in an upward direction, although the rows of plants and people standing on the base lines of the left and right sides of the pool are drawn in opposite directions from each other and appear to have been drawn in a "sideways" position. (They are meant to be upright.) The aspect of this drawing that marks it as transitional are the figures in the bottom row, which now take the same direction as those in the upper row.

In fig. 549, a garden scene from ancient Egypt includes a lower row of trees on the bottom edge of the painting and in the same direction as the trees on the upper horizontal side of the pool. The row of small plants along the lower horizontal edge is also turned in the same direction. The plants on either side of the pool, however, are in opposite directions from each other. Here, as in fig. 548, images in some areas are in isolated and opposite directions while images in other areas follow the same direction.

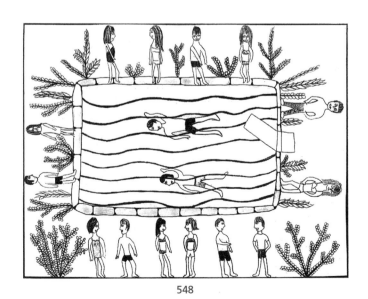

548

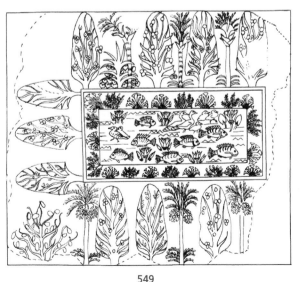

549

550

551

552

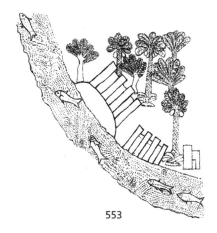

553

554

The trees in fig. 550 are placed in a unified direction, but the small plants along the winding path are on parallel base lines and in an opposite direction from the plants on the other side of the path. All of the plants, as with all figures on base lines in our previous examples, are perpendicular to their base lines. This is typical, whether base lines are straight or curved, horizontal, vertical, or diagonal. (Figs. 551 and 552 are examples of the few exceptions.)

Figs. 553 and 554 also demonstrate work that is at a transitional stage, but the organization of figs. 551 and 552 shows something new. In "The Party," the top row of girls is seated at the upper edge of the table. Opposite them are three table legs (each with three "feet") in the same direction. The girls on the left and right are perpendicular to their base lines, but their bodies curve upward. The girl who drew this picture felt compelled to show the girls on both sides of the table in an *almost* unified direction with the top

555

row of girls. Similarly, in the historical example in fig. 552, the towers curve upward from their base lines (the side walls). Both examples are unusual and interesting illustrations of the transition to complete unified directions of figures on base lines.

Eventually, in the art of older children, teenagers, and adults, and as we see in figs. 555-557, images are placed in a *unified direction* (the seated adults and children on two parallel base lines in fig. 555, the plants and birds on individual base lines in fig. 556, and the trees in fig. 557).

556

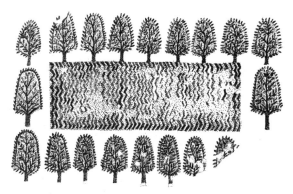

557

558

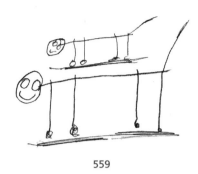

559

560

561

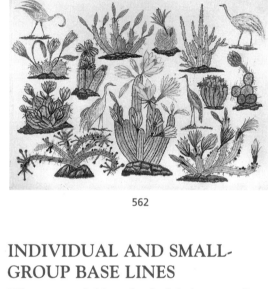

562

563

INDIVIDUAL AND SMALL-GROUP BASE LINES

When some children (and adults) eventually decide to place their images on several different levels, they can no longer use common base lines and must place individual lines beneath each figure. The lines drawn beneath each figure soon give way to more subtle and sophisticated devices: grass, shadows, rocks, and so on provide the necessary visual stability (see figs. 558-562). Often, as in fig. 561, there is a need for more than one type of baseline. This will depend on the artist's need to vary the objects' horizontal and vertical positions and on the placement of figures in relation to one another (figs. 563-566).

564

565

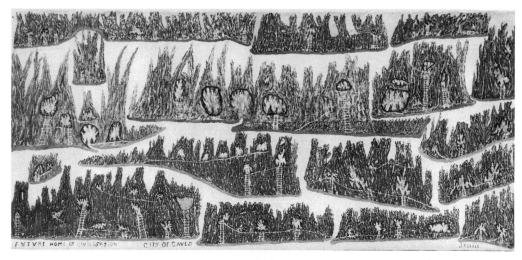

566

CONSCIOUSNESS OF ARTISTIC FORM

567

568

569

570

571

572

IMPLIED BASE LINES

An earlier example of implied base lines was cited in fig. 524, where rows of grass in one quadrant give the impression and have the effect of baselines. In his pen full of roosters (fig. 567), Paul drew and painted these figures in rows on implied base lines. (Although he showed one rooster on a baseline of grass, lower right, he evidently did not feel the need to repeat this.) An artist subconsciously creates an optical illusion of a kind when he or she places figures in rows and close together so that, in this case, our minds "see" horizontal lines beneath the roosters' feet. Figs. 568-572 also demonstrate this effect. The page from the *Codex Nuttal*, an ancient painted manuscript (fig. 573), is interesting because it shows an artist who was at a transition stage between implied baselines and no baselines at all, implied or actual. See how the glyphs in the upper right corner are placed here and there—not in even rows—and lack the clearly defined bottom edge that is seen elsewhere in the painting.

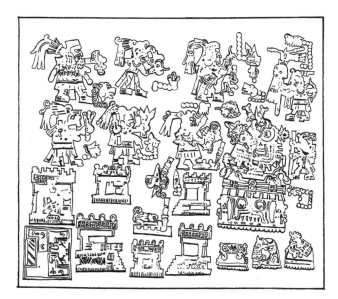

573

574

575

CLOSE JUXTAPOSITIONS WITH NO BASE LINES

In fig. 574 there are no base lines, but the numerous figures are in such close juxtaposition that there can be no illusion that they are "floating," and no grass or other differentiation of the ground is necessary. Notice how, in their hand-to-hand combat, some of the Indians and soldiers overlap. While overlapping was described in an earlier chapter as a separate stage, that was just one example of how various stages are interrelated—in this case overlapping and the placement of figures in relation to one another. Base lines and directions of figures are another example of such interrelationships. The employment of one may lead to the use of another. (Also see fig. 575 for another example of close juxtaposition.)

SUMMARY

Through examples of drawings, paintings, and other media by children, adults, and ancient artists, we have examined various spatial orientations and placements of figures in pictorial space. The uses of baselines to anchor figures, closely juxtaposed figures without baselines, overlapping, and isolated and unified direction have been discussed, as well as the interrelationship of different artistic factors.

The subject of figures' spatial orientation will be continued in the next chapter but with the focus on depth and the means used to indicate it.

CHAPTER SEVEN

Spatial Depictions

576

577

FIGURES ON FOREGROUND PLANES

Until they are able to depict depth, artists simply place figures in the foreground of their work. The boy who drew the house and trees in fig. 576 was able to conceptualize the house as a whole. By showing not only the front and roof but also both sides, he was expressing his own artistic conception, not copying what could actually be seen. In a sense, he created his own reality of the house, learning much more from that than if he had merely copied. The houses and trees in fig. 577 were done by a man who had never had lessons and who, when he had some leisure time later in life, began to draw at the stage he had left off as a child. Each house sits on its own base line (one near the top, which looks as if it is using a barn roof for a base line, was simply placed too close to the barn by the artist), and each front determines the direction of the left and right sides. He was just emerging from a transitional stage: the diagonal direction of some of the trees is determined by the upper corners of the island.

The German folk art in figs. 578 and 579, the beds in figs. 580 and 581, the bus or car in fig. 582, and Donald's flute (fig. 583) demonstrate similar configurations. (Two historical examples are provided in figs. 584 and 585 for comparison.)

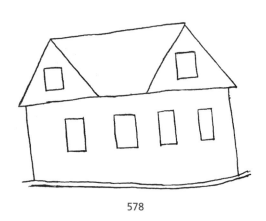

578

579

580

581

582

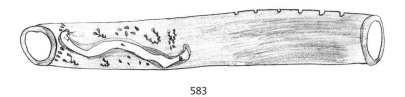

583

584

585

586

587

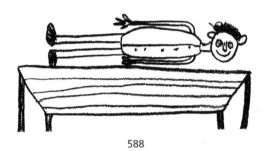

588

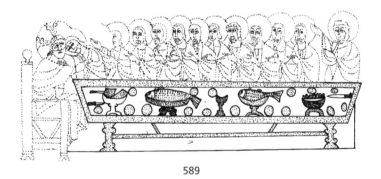

589

DIAGONAL LINES AND DEPTH

Instead of using base lines and flat planes, some older children and adults try to show images extending back into space. Their concern for depth is apparent when they use diagonal lines, intended to give a three-dimensional effect, in depictions of rectangular subjects. Some children depict rectangular forms with the sides slanted inward and downward so that opposite angles are equal but in reverse directions (fig. 586). Anne's idea for showing all of the table legs attached at the corners is only one of several ways this can be done. Notice that her table is wider above than below, like Donald's in fig. 587 or the bed of Karl's drawing (fig. 588). Of the many historical examples of similar solutions, figs. 589-591, and 594 are representative. Note also that in both figs. 588 and 590, the reclining human figures appear to float above the couch and bier because the artists were not at a stage where they could conceive of overlapping.

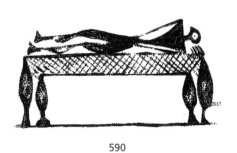

590

591

592

593

594

Connie drew an apartment house (fig. 592), using the bottom edge of the paper as the base line for three sides of the building and employing equal and reversed angles with the roof to give the impression of depth. An older boy made the roof in his drawing (fig. 593) the same as Connie's, but the building sides are diagonal and parallel to the sides of the roof, not on the baseline formed by the bottom of the building. This is a step forward in visual conceptual development. (A similar solution appears in fig. 594.) The sides of the buildings of Rockefeller Center (fig. 595) are visible, but the diagonal lines of the roof setbacks and two sides of the base are convergent, which indicates a yet more advanced understanding of how to indicate depth in pictorial space.

595

596

597

598

599

THE TRANSITION TO PARALLEL LINE RELATIONSHIPS

Many artists try to show an object's depth by representing its sides with near-parallel diagonal lines. This is a transition to the use of fully parallel diagonal lines. Only one side of the cabinet in the drawing by Karen, fig. 596 can be seen, and the diagonal lines of the top are not parallel. Mary shows almost parallel lines for the long sides of the bed in fig. 597, and figs. 598 and 599 are historical counterparts to the girls' drawings. Figs. 600-602 show parallel lines in one portion of the drawing or painting but not everywhere they could be applied.

At another stage, opposite sides of an individual rectangular image are parallel, but there is no unity of direction among the lines in other images in the same composition. The 13-year-old boy who drew "Our Dining Room" (fig. 603) was beginning to see parallel line relationships in the

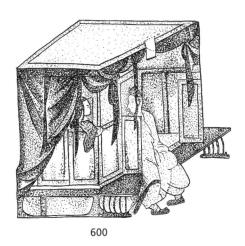

600

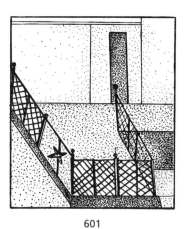

601

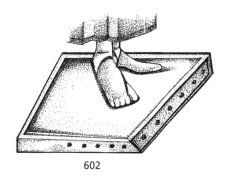

602

603

separate pieces of furniture, but he was unable to bring them into a unified structure. Fig. 604 is a historical example of this: there is no directional relationship between the figures, although parallel lines are used in each individually. (Figs. 605-607 are additional examples.)

Finally, although Richard didn't quite achieve a unified direction (fig. 608), he must have been striving for that in the parallel lines of his chairs and chessboard.

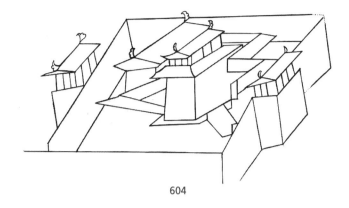

604

605

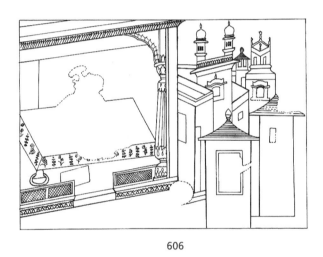

606

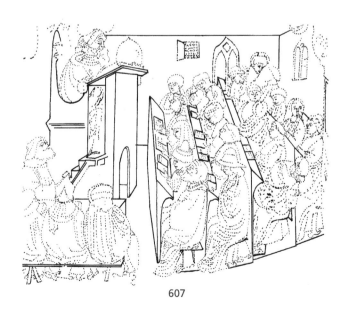

607

608

609

610

ACHIEVING UNITY OF DIRECTION

The direction of the lines in all of the objects in the mechanical drawing class (fig. 609)—drawing tables, papers, stools—is one. The diagonal outlines of the tables and stools are parallel. The drawing in figs. 610 and 611 may look somewhat stiff, but it shows that the boys had created a gestalt formation through their own initiative and judgment. Parallel diagonal lines are a natural stage in early pictorial expression that allows artists to show depth. At what some believe is a more advanced stage, the diagonal lines are no longer parallel and tend to converge in the distance at what is known as a "vanishing point." The parallel diagonal lines in fig. 611 also provide a more convincing conception of "sitting." Figs. 612 and 613 are historical examples, and the aerial views of towns in figs. 614-616 are excellent examples of unified parallel relationships. The boy who drew "An Airplane over a Small Town" (fig. 615) was exceptionally aware of the relationships of houses to each other and to the streets and of the airplane to the streets. Notice how the direction and tilt of the plane relate to the direction of the houses and streets and how precisely the body, tail, and right wing are arranged so that the entire airplane is visible.

611

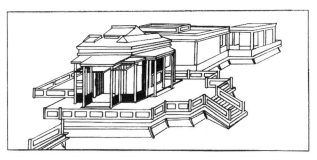

612

613

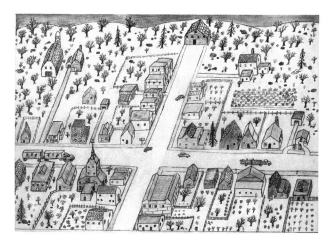

614

615

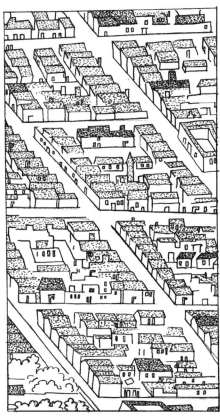

616

SUMMARY

We have described and illustrated various transition stages in line relationships to show depth in pictorial space: objects on foreground planes, diagonal lines, parallel lines, figures with equal opposite angles in reversed directions, and nearly and completely parallel relationships among objects. From these examples, we saw that children and other artists often obtained their desire to show depth without using vanishing-point perspective.

In chapter 8 we will study line, shape, and figure-ground spatial relationships in drawings of the head and facial features.

CHAPTER EIGHT

Development of
Face and Eye

617

618

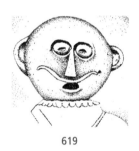

619

620

The head and face, with the eye and other features, are usually thought to be the most important visible aspects of a human or animal, and for this reason they have been reserved for a separate chapter. Even in the earliest conceptions of a human drawn or painted by a young child, one soon sees eyes, a mouth, and usually a nose placed in the circular outline of the "head-body." Here we will look at the relationships of the facial features to one another, the movement of the features to one extended side to indicate direction, the differentiation of the extended side into forehead, nose, etc., and the development of the eye.

DIRECTION OF FACIAL FEATURES IN RELATION TO HEAD

Looking first at horizontal-vertical relationships and using Carda's drawing (fig. 617) as our first example, we see that the round eyes, eyebrow, and mouth in her picture are perpendicular to the nose. While some children might draw a circular nose, the horizontal-vertical structure is still apparent, and it is even more obvious when the nose has a vertical shape (figs. 618 and 619). A more advanced conception by Leni (fig. 620) and historical comparisons in figs. 621-624 show the same relationship. Note that in contrast to the earlier stage shown in figs. 617 and 618, each eye in these examples is elongated and has pointed corners.

In figs. 625-629, we see a different relationship: the eyes appear to follow the curvature of the head, and this in turn changes the direction of angles between the eyes and nose. The desire to follow the curve of the face by slanting the eyes probably led to this stage.

In fig. 630 the eye's conformity to the curve of the face is gone: now the eyes slant upward. One might argue that they are in a horizontal-vertical relationship to the outline of the face, but the dominant characteristic is the features' variable directions. The same pattern is shown in figs. 631-634.

621

622

623

624

625

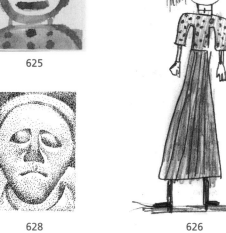

626

627

628

629

630

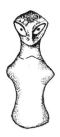

632

633

634

631

FACES AND VARIABLE DIRECTIONS

With regard to faces, variable directions and angles do not necessarily indicate a higher degree of sophistication in the artists and their works. Some European masters, for example, often used the horizontal-vertical configuration.

635

636

INDICATION OF DIRECTION

We have seen how children move from symmetrical images of the human being—one arm and one leg on each side of the body surmounted by a round or even rectangular head—to less symmetrical forms that show direction and suggest movement. For example, both arms may extend to one side; both feet may be turned in one direction. The head or face may show a simple extension in the side, which may suggest "nose," even though the nose is drawn in the center of the face. If this nose is omitted, however, the horizontal-vertical structure is destroyed. Children, and other artists, now look for a new relationship, and the only one that seems possible is reversion to the concentric circular image. Billy's drawing (fig. 635) shows two eyes and an extension of one side of the face with no nose in the center. This is a transition stage between the more symmetrical and static form and the asymmetrical, dynamic form that shows direction and the illusion of motion. Billy, in this example, wanted to maintain the central location of the eyes, with the mouth beneath them relating to the lower curve of the face. But he also is becoming aware of the concept of looking or turning the head to one side. This transitional solution is widespread in the history of art (see figs. 636-638).

637   638

639

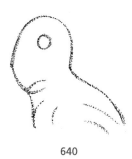

640

641

642

643

644

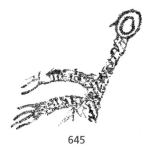

645

646

647

648

While both eyes may be drawn initially by the child who wants to show a sideways direction, soon one eye will be omitted. Alice's drawing (fig. 639) is an admirable solution. The eye is placed in the center of the head for visual clarity according to primary figure-ground relationships; that is, it has a clear, empty ground all around it (also see figs. 640-642). In these examples the original horizontal-vertical relationship of eyes, nose, and mouth has been abandoned, and a new relationship has been achieved.

In the next phase, we can see differentiation in the extension of one side of the face or head. In figs. 643 and 644, Paul and Donald drew definite noses extending from one side. (Paul also has drawn extensions that indicate chin and lips.) Varying numbers of differentiated extensions can likewise be seen in figs. 645-651 from various periods in Europe and Africa. The round eyes in all of these figures remain in the center of the head.

649

650

651

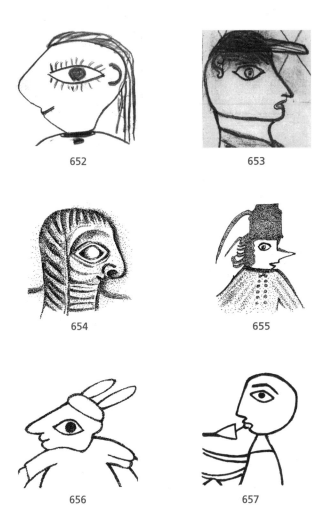

652

653

654

655

656

657

In figs. 652 and 653 we see something new. Elizabeth and Thomas felt the necessity to change the shape of the eye. These are also examples of what some researchers refer to as the "staring eye." Such eyes appear to be staring only because the pupils are at a primary stage of figure-ground relationships where they, as figures, are clearly set off from the ground areas of the eyeballs with no overlapping. The elongated eye remains in the center of the head, while differentiated extensions appear on the sides. Thomas has shown a definite nose, upper and lower lips, and chin. The historical comparisons (figs. 654-656) show similar eye shapes in the center of the head, but in fig. 657 the eye is closer to the differentiated side.

In the next developmental step we see that the corner of the eye touches and is perpendicular to the forehead outline. Although the eye and mouth may take different directions, they will be placed similarly in relation to the outlined face (fig. 658). The same relationships are seen in figs. 659-661, but in fig. 662 we see that the mouth is parallel to the jaw line but not to the eyes (also see figs. 663-665).

Although the eyes in figs. 666-669 are near the foreheads, we see that their rounded shape has influenced the forehead shape. When eyes are

658

659

660

661

662

placed near the forehead, it is more common to see the elongated shape, however.

Eventually, as our artistic conceptions develop in visualizing the face, the eye and the mouth become parallel to one another and perpendicular to the differentiated outline. The indentation where the eye meets the outline marks the bottom point of the forehead and the starting point of the nose. Figs. 670-672 show these characteristics. The parallel relationship between the eye and mouth is also seen in figs. 673-675 and 681-693.

The development of the head and facial features extends to animals: in the faces of the dog and horse in figs. 676 and 677, the eyes are parallel to the mouths and to the upper borders of the muzzles and jaw lines.

663

664

665

666

667

668

669

670

671

672

673

674

675

676

677

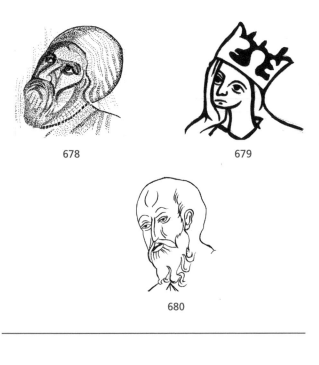

678

679

680

681

682

683

684

685

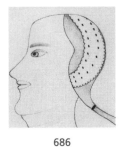

686

TRANSITION STAGE

In their attempt to show the head and face fully and clearly while simultaneously expressing the idea of looking or facing sideways, artists may show both eyes and both sides of the face but with one side only partially visible. This transitional "three-quarter" view, as it is sometimes called, is seen in figs. 678-680, which also share two complete eyes of equal shape and size and symmetrical mouths. The noses in all are similar to those that have been formed by extending one portion of the facial outline (see p. 113).

DEVELOPMENT OF THE EYE

The simplest form of the eye, the dot, (fig. 637) is replaced by the circular or oval shape (figs. 636, 640, 641, 645, and 649), which very soon contains another shape, the round pupil (figs. 617-619, 635, 639, 642-644, 646-648, and 651). Gradually the eye shape becomes more oval, or elongated (figs. 625-627, 630, 632, 666, 668). The iris is usually centered. Figs. 624, 628, 629, 632, 634, 659, 663, and 664 show the elongated eye with pointed corners. Because many of these examples are from sculptures, there are no pupils. The eyes in figs. 633, 638, 652-657, 661, 662, 665, 667, 676, and 677 are elongated, with pointed corner, and the centered irises are for the most part set off clearly from the white of the eye with no overlapping or touching. Irises that just touch the eyelid or are slightly overlapped by it are seen in figs. 620, 622, 623, 631, 658, 660, 670, 673, 674, and 680. All of the eyes cited have been described as "staring" eyes, because the irises' intensity when they are so starkly set off from their ground gives that impression. If the iris is placed closer to one corner of the eye, that corner will usually be nearest the forehead or side of the face to show direction (figs. 670, 674, 675, 679, 681-684). In 683-686, we find that the artist has added the pupil to the iris.

687

688

689

690

After indicating eye direction, the next step for the artist is to drop the small space or ground area between the iris and the corner of the eye that is closer to the nose/forehead area. This ground area, having been reduced as the iris was moved from its central position, loses its purpose. Now the iris, which may still be circular but usually becomes slightly elliptical, is placed at "the corner," which has been opened up and eliminated.

Nina's drawing (fig. 687) shows just such an eye. At this stage and at times at the last stage in the development of the eye, the eyelids overlap the white and the iris. In Nina's case, the eyelid has figural meaning: it is set off by the ground areas of the iris, the white of the eye, and the areas near the bridge of the nose and just below the eyebrow. When Nina set the pupil completely off from the iris, she reverted to the primary stage of figure-ground relationships. (Similar eyes can be seen in figs. 688-690.)

The length of the eye and eyelid appeared shortened with the advent of the nearly round iris, and this becomes even more pronounced as the iris becomes more elliptical and the eye and eyelids shorter still. A year after Nina made the drawing in fig. 687, she drew her self-portrait (fig. 691). We see more differentiation in the outline of the face, with the thinner upper lip, subtle curves of the nose, and more shading of both figural and ground areas around the forehead and hair, curls, jaw and neck, and upper eyelid. The extreme ellipse of the eye and iris are also seen in figs. 692 and 693.

691

692

693

SUMMARY

We have seen how the clearest conception of the head and face, with two eyes, a nose, and a mouth all centrally placed in a symmetrical and usually perpendicular relationship, gradually changes to a more asymmetrical structure in which one eye and the mouth are placed closer and closer to one side of the head. We have purposely avoided the terms "side view" and "profile," because they imply a single viewpoint and not a holistic conception. It is true that artistic conceiving closely approaches single viewpoint imagery at this point, but there are subtle differences of completeness and interfunctional unity that are missing in the conceptually oriented single viewpoint. In a single-viewpoint drawing or painting, figure-ground relationships may be confused. The nose, mouth, and eyes may be disproportionate to one another: for example, a sharp, pointed nose next to a mouth with full, rounded lips and full eyelids and ears.

In the last chapter we will talk about guiding students in ways that will encourage the unfolding of their individual and inherent visual artistic abilities.

CHAPTER NINE

The Teaching Guide

In this chapter you will find a description of methods that will encourage your students—or your own children, if you are a parent—to express their ideas pictorially in their own ways, step by step, from simple to more complex stages of expression. The procedure, which is very much the same regardless of the student's age, will help children, adolescents, and adults create genuine pictorial statements that conform to their mental and emotional natures. *The artistic form is within everyone's reach, although talent determines its power and richness.*

GUIDANCE FOR CHILDREN

It is clear, if we watch young children's progress with speech or climbing stairs or handling a spoon, that they develop their skills gradually, naturally, and at their own pace. They don't require instruction in the rules of speech: no one says, "Lily, now we are going to learn to talk. Our first lesson will be 'da-da' and 'ma-ma.' " By the same token, children also have all the "rules" for artistic expression within themselves. But because they usually don't have the opportunity to see people drawing every day, or even occasionally, they may need a little encouragement—in the form of adult interest and the right tools—to begin. Before we explore the adult's role in children's artistic development, we need to understand the nature of young children's work.

Although we cannot call their first scribbles and structures "art," these expressions are important in their overall development. Children do not draw in order to make pictures but because they have an inner need. When their natural tendencies are allowed to blossom, they express themselves spontaneously using symbols that are universal archetypes. They want to make their images visible, and they draw or paint what they know and visualize, artistically and intuitively, more than what they see around them. Because their lives are centered on themselves, the outside world initially holds little interest. But their inner worlds are so clear to them that it is fruitless to tell them what to do artistically. Leave them alone as much as you can, and never ask, "What is it?" Children younger than seven should never be taught what to create. Adults need to be aware of the magical world in which children live and should avoid confusing them by introducing them too soon to the world of abstract adult concepts.

We need to be aware of another point as well. The stages of visual artistic growth in children that have been presented may give the impression that they all move in an orderly way from A to B and onward. But of course we simplify and generalize, and the reality is very different: children are sometimes tired and don't do all that they are capable of; they revert at times to an earlier stage and then return to their latest achievements; they may be disturbed by events at home or school and unable to dedicate themselves to their artwork. Teachers need to be aware of such intervening factors.

IMITATION AND OTHER DETRIMENTAL EXPRESSIONS

When guiding children from the age of seven upward, adults need to look first for the particular quality of artistic formation that already exists in their minds. Are the children's pictures imitations of nature, copies from in front of an object, imitations of popular cartoon or comic strip characters, or genuine expressions? Imitation always means that the artwork does not conform with the child's visual understanding. It also lacks the interfunctional relationships that bring all parts of the picture together as a whole.

The same is true of a reproductive memory picture. Children try to "re-collect," or put together, unrelated images in a piecemeal manner, with the result that their pictures fall apart visually. Such a memory picture is often a chaotic thing.

Some children may produce creative expressions or accidental effects that lack unity of artistic form. The author calls this *self-expression*, which John Dewey, the educational philosopher, described as "spewing forth."

Genuine development starts with a simple unified structure that gradually becomes more and more complex. By guiding students to evaluate (judge) their works, teachers may give them the procedures necessary for their own artistic self-evaluations. Using this method, the teachers set an example. This is the important point of this approach: developing in students the ability to evaluate their own work. It is also more difficult

than simply letting them do whatever they please or directing their every move while imposing adult rules and concepts.

When teachers are mainly interested in obtaining a "spontaneous" result from their students, they push the children to finish their work as fast as possible. This misunderstood pedagogical attitude reveals no knowledge of early intuitive visual conceiving and results in incomplete, hastily done pictures that achieve nothing.

Many children today do reproductive memory pictures or poorly organized self-expressions, but they need the time to contemplate, to dream, without any sense of hurry so that they may clearly visualize their inner images. It seems obvious that these quiet creative hours can have a powerful influence on other aspects of a child's life as well. A relaxed atmosphere combined with the teacher's guidance toward artistic self-evaluation will yield positive results.

A POSITIVE TEACHING TECHNIQUE

If children are confronted with their fragmented drawings and asked to comment, their resulting confusion can be helpful. *Consciousness of their confusion makes it necessary for them to clarify their thinking and find their own ways.* Most children are unused to this kind of self-analysis, and it can be a painful procedure at first. But they must see what is wrong by themselves. You can help by saying, for example, "Compare this part of the picture with that part." When students begin to see the confusion, they may be unpleasantly surprised, but again this is necessary. If you point out the mistake, your students will want to believe you, and this undermines their trust in themselves. Because all of your explanations are words of authority that children will accept, even if they are not convinced of their merit, be careful not to impose your own views.

A QUESTIONING STRATEGY

Children need to understand their pictures in order to digest the experiences, and if they cannot do this, you should seek all possible means to help them. They should be told to work as slowly as possible. If they are reproducing memory pictures, or if the pictures are chaotic, you may say, "Look at your pictures." Then ask, "Which part makes you happier?" "Which part do you like best?" Children can be helped to identify problem parts if the teacher asks, "Which part bothers you? Which part can you make better?" (The definition of "better" is left up to the child.)

You will need to improvise, to invent questions, to constantly direct children's perceptions and guide them to make comparisons. But never tell children what is wrong with their artworks. Lead them by questioning into seeing for themselves where the fault lies. They will soon discover it, and you will be amazed at the intelligence they show in judging their own work.

If the children continue to be confused, though, they should be asked to make silhouettes of their images with black ink. The contrast of the black ink on the white paper usually creates such a powerful impression that the errors suddenly leap to their attention. Alternatively, if they look at their drawings from a distance or upside down, shape or line relationships become more obvious.

Children are given the ability to see and to create artistic forms by nature, but teachers must know that it exists so that they can help foster it and provide the proper encouragement.

To help children find their way, you need to understand them as psychological phenomena: where have they come from, what are their interests? If the children in a large class come from many different environments, it is very difficult to teach. But even when there is no common background and the children live in different worlds, you can introduce them to general experiences common to all. "What did you have for breakfast? What did you see on your way to school? What did you do on Sunday?" Questions like these help stimulate visual memories.

If working with a class size that prohibits giving attention to each child, ask one child at a time to put his or her picture up on the wall or a bulletin board. Tell the others not to work but to look and listen carefully to Jack or Mary judge his or her picture, which should already be completed. As the child is led to judge his or her work and to discover any problems, the rest of the class can learn to judge by watching and listening.

You can ask, "Mary, how do you like your picture?" If she has trouble with her answer, you might ask, "Do you like the tree better or the cow better?" "Do you see something that bothers you?" Finally Mary is able to discover the problem and in this way determines for herself what changes need to be made. When this is done, tell the children that for the next 10 minutes they will all put their pictures in front of them and try to judge them. Do this for a month, and each student's artistic vision will improve considerably.

In a smaller class, the process is the same, but you can give more individual attention. Whenever the children have a problem in their art that is of general concern, the drawing should be put up and discussed before the class. *This discussion is between only you and the student whose work is displayed.* The others may ask questions but may not express any criticisms. Their comments are discouraged because all too often their remarks or questions can be distracting and unhelpful.

The prerequisite for progressive development is finding subjects that interest the children, and this is another reason for knowing their backgrounds. Ideally you would keep a record of such information: "Michael lives on Milvia Street with his mother and sister. He has a gray cat and a white dog." "Maria lives near the beach and likes boats and seagulls. She has two brothers." You need to make a commitment to gaining the information necessary to assess each child's emotional background.

Often, when studying a drawing, you will see that one part of the picture held a particular interest for a child and that he or she had consequently worked on it very diligently and enthusiastically. In succeeding pictures that grow from some such interest, you can suggest that children enlarge upon their themes, perhaps with more branches and leaves or flowers or birds in the tree. The tree, for example, can remain simple, but the differentiated contents may create a new challenge and further children's confidence in their achievements. Differentiation of a simple idea can be accomplished with any subject: what is most important is the children's intimate relation to their subjects. Only when they have discovered and attempted to solve their own pictorial problems can they obtain a clear visual conception of their pictures. To help accomplish this, the children should write comments on the back of each picture that describe the problem and how they intend to solve it. In a large group, 20 or more students, this kind of teaching can be done only if each child has a portfolio of his or her numbered and dated drawings and paintings that the teacher can take home for study.

Bringing objects into the classroom—a bird or stuffed animal, fruit, flowers, vegetables—can give children fresh ideas. The objects should be put away after there has been enough time for looking and touching so they don't simply try to reproduce what they have seen.

The author often brought art reproductions to class, and if these are on a level with the children's development, they can be very stimulating. Pictures need strong line directions and extended and directed figures, above, below, and beside each other with simple overlapping. In addition to folk art and ancient and aboriginal art, good examples can often be found in books on needlework, appliqué, and collage. At no time should the children be told to copy examples. Such art should be shown to individual children *only* after they have made a significant achievement in their own art. In this way their artistic vision is reinforced, and they gain insights into the example that might otherwise not be apparent.

In a well-integrated class, mural painting is an excellent and satisfying learning experience. Choose small groups of children (two to four) of about the same age and certainly on a similar developmental level and ask them to decide on a theme. Then let them make careful drawings before they begin painting. Each child will work out his or her part, and the entire painting will be a well-organized whole, completely understood by all. (See Appendix One for an example of group work.)

The necessity for discipline in a small class is rare, but with a group of 15 or more, there can be a problem. Keep the children interested! Help them to discover subjects and media that match their natures. Techniques and skills are secondary to the children's artistic conceptions. Pencils, crayons, and clay are preferred for children between the ages of six and eight, but it is best to limit the number of crayons to six, including the three primary colors. (Eventually the older children develop their awareness of values and intensities and demand a greater selection.) (Note 10)

Cardboard relief, printing, watercolor, and tempera painting can be provided for children between eight and 12. As most children's drawings are two-dimensional and drawn with clear outlined shapes, relief printing is a good medium. It is especially helpful to children who draw carelessly or have trouble organizing their pictures. The same is true for making low reliefs (or *bas-relief*) in oil-base modeling clay. Both printing and modeling require clarity of vision and subjects with which the children are familiar. A clear well-organized drawing should always precede such artistic endeavor. The author often told his students, "Outline your idea. Make many drawings until the idea gets into your bloodstream."

Clay can be used for three-dimensional productions or for reliefs modeled on a flat surface, although its malleability can lead to accidental effects. The consistency of the clay is important, because students need to be able to control it so that it doesn't sag or fall over while they are working with it.

Older students can carve soap, plaster-of-paris blocks, or soap stone. They can handle carving tools and the materials and in addition have the patience to work slowly. Of course, the use of carving tools must be closely supervised.

SOME DETRIMENTAL FACTORS

Some methods and materials should be avoided. Big brushes can be too difficult for small children to handle. Easels cause paint to run down the paper surface, and in trying to "erase" the drips, children merely create smears. Have them place their papers on tables or on the floor while painting. When a process is too slow and tedious—such as with mosaics and other sophisticated techniques—the children may not understand their pictures as integrated entities.

One of the chief causes of failure in art education is a frequent change of subject. Continuous change gives children little time for concentration on artistic formation, and if this continues they cannot progress. When they have completed five or six pictures with different subjects, ask them what they have to say about each picture. Their answers will be vague or confused, or they might say defiantly that all of their pictures are good. You need to say, "The pictures are all the same, and none of them is finished." Confronting the children with their failures will have a positive effect.

When one child imitates another's work, the imitator is frustrated and not working to his or level. If imitation continues, you must address the problem. "Don't you want to be Carl? Your name is Carl, not Joe. Maybe it is difficult to be Carl, but I will help you." Go back to the basic attribute of self-respect.

When children succeed in producing pictures in which all the parts are intrinsically related to the whole (a gestalt formation), when they can

see the whole picture at once and cannot change a single line or color, this is a great triumph for them and calls for praise—and even celebration. An occasional party encourages each student to make the effort to be the honored guest at the next festive occasion.

GUIDANCE FOR ADOLESCENTS

Adolescents will usually have been influenced by non-artistic teaching methods. To develop inherent potentialities in such cases, you must discover each student's particular stage of artistic conceiving. The process is like that with younger children.

The subject should be simple and should be related to individual experiences, and clear outline drawings should be the first step. Students are asked to identify what part of their work they like best. In succeeding pictures, their goal is to make their whole pictures as visually clear as the organized part in the first picture. Silhouettes can again be an aid to clear visual thinking and artistic cognition, and works of art from different epochs that relate to the students' own developments provide insights and enable them to understand their own potential.

GUIDANCE FOR ADULTS

In adult classes, the author rarely directed but guided by asking questions and tried to elicit each student's artistic uniqueness. He wished to gradually develop in adult students an understanding of basic art forms purged of all inessential details. He would often suggest that they find a theme inspired from former years but not a mere memory picture. The details of long-ago experiences were no longer readily accessible, but the images that arose from the unconscious often led to the creation of powerful pictorial works.

THE ROLE OF CRAFTS

While we have considered the gradual unfolding of a child's, a teenager's, or a layman adult's artistic forms, from simple to increasingly complex, these developments can also be applied to the creation of useful and visually pleasing craft objects. Craft creations help fix these forms in students' minds and can help to eliminate any superficial or overly detailed aspects of their work since such details can be too difficult to execute in a craft object. Also, for them to see their images achieve three-dimensional reality and to learn that these appeal to others helps them to experience a strong sense of reinforcement and social acceptance of their art.

SUMMARY

Regardless of whether you teach children, adolescents, or adults, you should understand each student and his or her interests, determine his or her stage of artistic form development, and then search out that quality that makes each student unique. This is the great challenge—to bring forth each student's unifying artistic form abilities, while not suppressing his or her individuality. Then one can say that the best kind of artistic creation can take place.

This book demonstrates the reality of artistic, gestalt form through hundreds of examples that also serve to validate the author's theory of visual, artistic conceiving. This was first presented in his book, The Unfolding of Artistic Activity, which was influenced by the theory of artistic consciousness proposed by Gustav Britsch, as Britsch's theory was expanded upon by Egon Kornmann, his foremost student.

This book is primarily about consciousness of artistic form and secondarily about art and art education, with the hope that these pages will inspire readers to seek connections between their own, their students', or their children's artistic form creations with works from around the world and down through the centuries. Gazing through this window to the rich heritage of the past and realizing the kinship of consciousness that unites us all, may we thus find a window to ourselves.

Plate 1

Eric, at 6 1/2 years of age, drew this picture of flowers. His picture clearly shows how he used the green grass blades to differentiate the spaces (ground areas) around the flowers. If he had not done so, he would have been confronted with big blank spaces of white paper. Although, he did not apply any prescribed rules of composition, his own inherent sense for unity of artistic form brought him to this realization.

Institute of Art Education, Berkeley, California

Plate 2

After doing a series of drawings of two fish, including one in which the fish crossed one another, Judd, at age 15 1/2 to 16 years of age, who was on the borderless transition stage of overlapping of figures, decided to stay with his earlier idea of the two fish placed in parallel curved positions. However, he simplified and enlarged the large leaves that form a ground area for the fish, and chose reddish hues for the leaves to further offset the blue and violet-beige figures of his fish. He also created some shading on the fish.

Institute of Art Education, Berkeley, California

Plate 3

Kenneth, like Judd (Plate 2), used large leaves to serve as a background for his frog. The large leaves were dictated by the size of the frog, and the details on the frog caused Kenneth to create details on the leaves. He, and the other youngsters whose artistic conceptions are shown in the color plates, were not told what to do. The same is true for the many children, teenagers and adults whose artworks are shown in the many black and white visuals in this book. Rather, Kenneth and the others were guided by challenging questions to evaluate their own artworks in order to discover parts that worked well, and parts that did not go well in their works. This teaching procedure is described in the last chapter.

Institute of Art Education, Berkeley, California

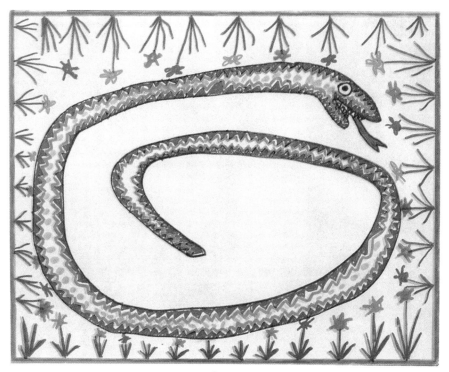

Plate 4a

Paul, in contrast to Adrienne (Plate 4b), added flowers around the outside of his snake's coil, but chose to keep the ground area within the coil empty. The border of flowers was added because he felt that the snake by itself looked "too powerful". The white paper within the coil did not bother him. He used bright primary colors (red, blue, and yellow) for the snake, and red for the flower blossoms. With such almost clashing colors, more colored details within the snake's coil would have been too much for him to see. That was his decision.

Insitute of Art Education, Berkeley, California

Plate 4b

Adrienne painted a picture of a snake, but found that the white paper around the snake made, in her words, "...a terrible clash....!" with her snake. So, she added plants, but then realized that she had to be very careful not to add too many plants. Still, things did not look right to her. Therefore, she added the spotty light brown sand and was fully satisfied with the result.

Institute of Art Education, Berkeley, California

Plate 5

Karen said about her painting of three girls, "...the design of the dresses are done in different shapes, the necklaces are also of different shapes. This explains why I had to paint the background in a more complex way than in my first picture.... After I painted the bushes, I felt the need to put in some colors because the green was too empty. I selected red and yellow blossoms....Now, the background fits in with the whole picture." This is an excellent statement by a student who was guided to make her own evaluation of the relationships of the various patterns and colors within her painting, and to arrive at her own solution. Such an experience is quite satisfying to art students, for it involves the very depths of their artistic beings.

Insititute of Art Education, Berkeley, California

Plate 6

Sherry, at 9 years of age, created a landscape with deer grazing in a clearing surrounded by trees. Whereas her deer are all placed in a unified direction (with "up" being toward the top of her paper), her trees are placed in several directions. She had not yet achieved a unity of direction of similar figures (the trees, in this case).

Institute of Art Education, Berkeley, California

Plate 7

Unlike Sherry (Plate 6), Eric, who created a picture of wild boars in a woods, placed all of the images (figures) in a unified direction. Eric, like Sherry, was on the primary stage of figure-ground relationships, with the figures placed side by side against a common empty ground area. In Plate 1, this same Eric, at a younger age, also was on the primary stage of such spatial relationships, and he was already on the stage of unified direction of figures. Note the individual base lines that Eric used in this "Boars in the Woods" picture in order to set each figure upon them.

Institute of Art Education, Berkeley, California

APPENDIX ONE

The subject of this picture is from the story of the country mouse and the city mouse: how they meet in a field of dandelions. It was done by a group of 20 eight-year-olds, who had been selected because their stages of development and their understanding of figure-ground, line, and color relationships were similar. Each child selected a theme—a group of dandelions, a city mouse, or a country mouse—that would be done with poster paints on 12 x 16-inch sheets of paper. After their paintings were finished, the pictures were glued together interchangeably— a group of dandelions with a group of mice—in a long row.

Close observation reveals that all figures— dandelions, mice, butterflies, and snails—are set off clearly from their empty grounds. Thus there is an overall visual order. Furthermore, the dandelions have vertical stems with leaves that branch out from the bottom at a slant. These figures were visually conceived, outlined, and directed and extended. Unified line direction has been added to figure and ground as another element of visual order. Mice, snails, and butterflies are also visualized as outlined directed figures that indicated various directions through the extensions of their shapes.

In their consciousness of colors, eight-year-old children are usually limited to a narrow variety of hues and values. As is evident here, they attempt to differentiate among the basic hues and values only when different meanings of objects or their parts require it. The overall distribution of hues and values, combined with the visual order, presents a well-established wholeness of form. Nothing can be changed without interfering with the total quality of the picture.

It is worth repeating that the children must be starting from the same developmental stage if a satisfactory result is to be achieved from such cooperative projects. Without the appropriate foundation, the children will be working together only in a superficial sense, and unrelated forms and disorganized shapes will give their work an accidental appearance.

One child may express his idea of a particular object in a completely different way than his companions; early stages of visual conceiving will appear beside later ones or next to memory images or imitative renderings. When children involved in a group art activity are not at a similar stage, the usual result is visual confusion.

To avoid such a result, the children's artistic solutions were thoroughly prepared, first by clarifying their vision. Because children commonly build their worlds of inner imagery by intense contact with objects, dandelions and pictures of dandelions were brought to class for study. The children plucked off the petals and discovered the various yellows in each blossom and the tiny bowl-shaped flower base that was supported by a thick stem. Some children found out that the stem contained a milky fluid. They observed the general shape of the leaves and how they branched off from the stem at a slant. In their own ways, some children further differentiated the dandelions' characteristics, but in the end they all shared a general conception of the flower and its parts.

Next they discussed the mice. In the story, they had been "impersonated" and would have to be drawn as little mice people. How should their dresses, jackets, and pants look? Some children needed to draw their ideas on the chalkboard. The final discussion concentrated on the heads. Which child had drawn the best shape? There was the elementary circular shape but also comparisons with the related shapes of different objects—potatoes and large radishes, for example. Different subjects with similar structures were again drawn with colored chalk.

Only after such preliminary clarifications are complete should children select and carry out their subjects. The entire task requires several hours, and hard work and concentration are required from both teacher and students. Genuine satisfaction and enjoyment follow, when each child realizes his or her contribution to the group's endeavor.

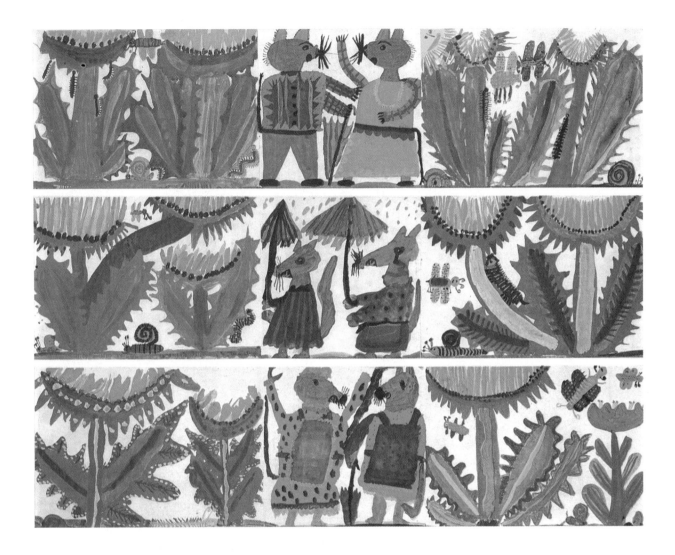

The three rows of mice, plants, and insects, done by a group of twenty 8 year old children are actually details of a long, continuous mural depicting a story of a city mouse who visited a country mouse. Each child could select his or her theme: a group of dandelions, or a pair of the mice to be done with poster paints on sheets of 12" x 16" paper. When done, the sheets were glued into one long one, with alternating panels, dandelions, mice, dandelions, etc. Because all of the children were on the same primary stage of figure-ground relationships, the same stage of color usage, and the same stage of variability of line direction, an overall unity of the mural was achieved. Without considering what stages of art development a group of children have in common before doing a cooperative mural, the result would be at best accidental, and lacking in visual unity.

Institute of Art Education, Berkeley, California

APPENDIX TWO

THREE DRAWINGS OF TWO FISH BY JUDD

These three drawings of two fish, by Judd, age 14, showing a progression from #1 to #3, led finally to the painting which he did, as shown in color Plate 2, found on page 127 of this book. Usually, students at the Institute of Art Education were encouraged to develop their artistic conceptions in drawings before doing paintings, because working with colors can bring forth new problems to be solved, and if the spatial orientation, location and other aspects of the overall form are not solved first of all in drawings, the students will be confronted with almost insurmountable obstacles.

1

2

3

1

2

3

4

A TEENAGER'S DEVELOPMENT WITH SCULPTURES

These four sculptured heads were done by Stuart, between age 12 1/2 years and 13 years of age. He was guided by questions to observe each work, to compare parts, to identify successful parts, and to identify problem parts, if any. He was asked if he could improve things in a next version? Answering in the affirmative, he went ahead to do so. Notice how Head 1 is really no more than a rather flat face. Head 2 shows curvature, and a hair mass. Head 3 shows that he added more hair, with texture and a neck. Finally in Head 4, he rounded the head more, gave the forehead more room, and also defined the nose and lips more. At this point he was entirely satisfied with his last (fourth) version. See Chapter 9 for a presentation of the recommended art teaching approach, which approach is also presented here and there in the other chapters of this book.

Institute of Art Education,
Berkeley, California

NOTES

Foreword
Note 1   Kornmann's German text was translated by a teacher of German in the United
                States, and that translation was Anglicized by Kerwin Whitnah, an art teacher
                and former student of Schaefer-Simmern's in California.

Chapter 1
Note 2   Henry Schaefer-Simmern referred to the emergence of spirals and circle-like
                figures from the early motor scribbles. However, visual judgment, as he indicated,
                is first clearly shown when the young child places his or her scribble entirely on
                the paper. That marks the very beginning of "figure-ground" relationships and is a
                valid visual, artistic judgment.

Note 3   The terms figure and ground come from Gestalt psychology. Applied to visual art,
                a "figure" is an intentional statement, and a "ground" is its pictorial background.
                The ground sets off a figure by making it visible by contrast. See Chapter 5,
                which specifically addresses figure-ground relationships, and Note 9 of that chap-
                ter.

Chapter 2
Note 4   Circle-like images with radiating straight-like lines show an important visual real-
                ization of a hitherto unrealized line-and-angle relationship, the horizontal and
                vertical (also called "the greatest contrast of direction") relationship described in
                the following text.

Note 5   The beginning of horizontal-vertical line relationships is a fundamental stage
                because now the child (or aboriginal artist, etc.) can develop new possibilities
                beyond the limitations of curvilinear forms. First realized where the segmented,
                "straight" lines meet the outlines of circle-like or oval images, the new relation-
                ships also are applied to images' extremities.

Note 6   By eliminating some radiating lines, the child uses the remaining ones to express
                the meaning of legs and arms, trunks and branches, etc. He or she certainly sees
                more parts of these subjects and knows conceptually many things about them. Yet
                it appears that the stage of gestalt, artistic form development determines what is
                drawn or painted and how it is done.

Note 7   Reversion: going back to an earlier stage of artistic form development in order to solve a visual problem with a particular subject. In the case cited, the child reverted to her earlier circular images with radiating lines to express hands.

Chapter 3
Note 8   The tree drawings with blossoms and birds (figs. 300-303) were done by four 10-year-olds. They are very good examples of how personality differences are reflected in work done by children who are on the same stage of visual conceiving, or artistic form development. It is the dynamic interplay of these drawings' unity of artistic form and their individual differences that is the fascinating reality of artistic, visual conceptions. When we lose attunement with our own visual, gestalt powers of consciousness, our individual differences may be expressed but will lack the holistic forms of visual conceptions.

Chapter 5
Note 9   The first use of the terms figure and ground is attributed to the Danish psychologist Edgar Rubin in his book, Visuell wahrgenommene Figuren, which was published in Copenhagen in 1921. Like other Gestalt theorists, Rubin was intrigued by how we perceive what we see; the well-known dictum that the whole is greater than the sum of its parts was the cornerstone of Gestalt thinking. Rudolf Arnheim's respected work, Art and Visual Perception (1954), also explored the significance of the figure-ground relationship.

Chapter 9
Note 10   Little has been mentioned in this book about the use of color and its development in relation to artistic form, but surely it is as important a means of artistic expression as lines, shapes, and spatial relationships. Henry Schaefer-Simmern referred to color in a general way for he believed that line direction and outlined shapes and their figure-ground relationships were of fundamental importance. However, he did believe, based on his research, that young children usually prefer to use primary and secondary hues with strong value contrasts and that secondary and tertiary hues, lighter contrasts, and less saturation come with more experience and sophistication. He contrasted the limited palettes of ancient Egyptian artists with the far fuller palettes of more modern artists.

ADDENDUM

Those Who Exchanged Ideas with, or Influenced Henry Schaefer-Simmern

Conrad Fiedler   German philosopher of art (1841-1895), friend of the Painter Hans von Maree, and the sculptor, Adolph Hildebrand. Only one book of Fiedler's writings, *Über die Beurteilung von Werken der bildenden Kunst* (1876), was translated into English as *On Judging Works of Visual Art,* (1948) by Schaefer-Simmern, H., and Mood, F. (University of California Press, Berkeley, CA). Schaefer-Simmern based his philosophy of art and artistic cognition on Fiedler's ideas.

Gustaf Britsch   Art educator and director of the Gustaf Britsch Institut für Kunstwissenschaft und Kunsterziehung, in Starnberg, south of Munich, in Germany. His book, *Theorie der bildenden Kunst* (1926) presented his research and ideas about artstic consciousness, which were based on the art philosophy of Conrad Fiedler.

Egon Kornmann   Foremost student of Gustaf Britsch, Kornmann continued Britsch's work after the latter's death, and published among other books, *Kunst im Leben (1954) Grundprinzipien bildnerischer Gestaltung* (1962). It was Kornmann's lectures on Britsch's theory that Schaefer-Simmern heard while in Prague in pre-Nazi days, and upon which the latter built his own newly formed theory of artistic activity. Kornmann and Schaefer-Simmern stayed in contact over the years, and Kornmann wrote the Foreword to the present book.

John Dewey   Noted educational philosopher and pragmatist, who wrote the Foreword to Schaefer-Simmern's book, *The Unfolding of Artistic Activity* (1948). Dewey wrote to philosopher Martin Schütze, "A meeting with Henry Schaefer-Simmern...came off today...it was the most exciting intellectual experience I had in many years."

Martin Schütze   Philosopher and author of *Academic Illusions in the Field of Letters and the Arts* (1933) which he published through the University of Chicago Press. Schütze was a good friend of Schaefer-Simmern, whom he addressed as "Meinem lieber Fruende Heinrich" ("My dear friend Henry"). We believe Schütze introduced John Dewey to him.

Bruno Adriani   Former director of schools in pre-Nazi East Prussia, Germany. Schaefer-Simmern referred to him as "My boss from East Prussia." Adriani visited Schaefer-Simmern's art classes in the town of Simmern, near the River Rhine, and was so impressed that he arranged for an exhibit of his students' art in Berlin. Adriani left Germany in the early 30s and settled in Carmel, California. He published a book, *Problems of the Sculptor* in 1943, through the Nierendorf Gallery in New York City.

Thomas Munro   Former director of the Cleveland Museum of Art, Munro wrote the introduction to the exhibition catalog for Schaefer-Simmern's exhibit of students' art at the Nierendorf Gallery, in New York City. Munro also arranged for a series of lectures at the Cleveland Museum of Art for Schaefer-Simmern.

Rudolf Arnheim   Gestalt psychologist specializing in perception and art, Arnheim met Schaefer-Simmern in New York city, and they kept in contact over the years. Among Arnheim's publications are: *Art and Visual Perception* (1954) and *Visual Thinking* (1969).

Seymour B. Sarason	Psychologist specializing in the area of the mentally handicapped, Sarason was the staff psychologist at the Southbury Training School, Southbury, Connecticut, when Schaefer-Simmern conducted research there, funded by the Russell Sage Foundation of New York City, with Selma and other mentally retarded women. Sarason, who later referred to Schaefer-Simmern as "my mentor," wrote extensively of the latter's research at Southbury Training School in Sarason's books: *Psychological Problems in Mental Deficiency* (1949) pp. 316-321, and *Psychological and Mental Retardation: Perspectives in Change* (1985) pp. 123-127.
Ed Taylor	Artist and collector of Pre-Columbian art of Mexico, Ed Taylor was a close friend of Schaefer-Simmern's. He made numerous trips to Mexico to collect mostly Tarascan ceramic pottery and images.
Rhoda Kellogg	While not a friend, but rather a colleague in the field of art of young children, Rhoda Kellogg was director of the Golden Gate Nursery School in San Francisco. Having accumulated many drawings and paintings of young children at her school, she then published a book listed in the reference section of the present book. Schaefer-Simmern reproduced four of her photographs of these children's artworks in Chapter 1, and 14 of them in Chapter 2 of the present book. The editors are grateful to her for giving permission to Schaefer-Simmern to reproduce them.

Some Former Students at the University of California, Berkeley

Helen Thaler Bob Simmons	Both Helen and Bob were members of a group carrying on the ideas of their mentor, Henry Schaefer-Simmern. The group met in some rooms above a small gymnasium in Berkeley. Later, Bob, who was in the Navy, collected art objects from China, Southeast Asia, and Japan, which were later sold to the Freer Gallery in Washington, DC. He resides now in Baltimore, Maryland.
Jay Frierman Heather Anderson	Kept in contact with Henry Schaefer-Simmern over the years.

Some Former Students in New York City

Mildred Hennert (Taylor)

	Mildred went on to earn her doctoral degree with Viktor Lowenfeld, at Penn State University, although she said to Schaefer-Simmern that her heart was not in it since she did not agree with Lowenfeld's ideas on art education. She became a professor at UCLA, married Ed Taylor, and joined him in collecting Tarascan art from Mexico.
Gudren Egeberg	Schaefer-Simmern married her in NYC and they both later went to Berkeley when he became a visiting professor at the university there. Her artworks appear in his book, *The Unfolding of Artistic Activity*. Later they divorced.

Some Students in the University of Minnesota Summer Theory Class of 1949

Roy E. Abrahamson	Mentioned below
Donald Waldoch	Mentioned below
Betty Emerson	Mentioned below
Stanley Wold	Later, Stan became a research leader of the National Art Education Association
William Boyce	Later became an important member of the Association for National Art Museums
Ken Thompson	
Ruth Falkenburg	
Bill Angelo	
June Alison	
Jim Fotia	
John Langen	
Louis Willie	An active artist
Reg Gilbertson	
Rev Robinson	Resides in New England, active as a watercolor artist
Geri Frise	

Some Former Full-Time and Part-Time Students at the Institute of Art Education, Berkeley

Roy E. Abrahamson Donald Waldoch Betty Emerson	Abrahamson, Waldoch and Emerson, as graduates in art education from the University of Minnesota, Minneapolis, traveled to Berkeley, California, to be the first day time students at the new Institute of Art Education, established by Schaefer-Simmern in September, 1949
Wayne Anderson	Professor of Art History, MIT
Ernst Stolz	Formerly a draftsman, he studied at the Institute of Art Education and was a practicing artist specializing in painting.
Elisa Stinson	Originally a member of a class of layman adults taught by Schaefer-Simmern in San Francisco, Elisa then came to study at the Institute in Berkeley.
David Green	David, like Elisa, came to the Institute for spring term 1950, as a painter.

Some Layman Students at the Institute of Art Education, in Berkeley

John Alsberg	Delivered the eulogy at the funeral of Schaefer-Simmern, who died on October 16, 1978
Kerwin Whitnah	Artist and teacher, he became an active, dedicated supporter of Schaefer-Simmern
Sally Whitnah	Wife of Kerwin, later divorced
Sylvia Fein	Artist, and later also author, Sylvia beame a dedicated follower of Henry Schaefer-Simmern.
Gertrude Washburn Conley	She married Henry Schaefer-Simmern
Clement J. Renzi	Formerly an accountant, Clement became a sculptor of some note.
Hilda Present Lewis	She became a professor of elementary education at California State University, San Francisco, and an active member of the National Art Education Association

Some Students in Henry Schaefer-Simmern's Classes in San Francisco

Annette Rosenschein, Ruth Haas Lilienthal, Delia Fleishhacker Ehrlich,
Bella Gerstle Fleishhacker, Delia Fleishhacker Ehrlich, Elise Stern Haas

Others Who Supported Henry Schaefer-Simmern's Work

Hilda Present Lewis	Published a eulogy honoring Schaefer-Simmern, shortly after his death.
Diana Korzenik	Professor of Art Education, and an active member of the research section of the National Art Education Association. She also published a eulogy when Schaefer-Simmern died.
Alfred Frankenstein	Noted art critic, he published a eulogy when Schaefer-Simmern died.
John Michael	Professor Emeritus of Art Education, Miami Univeristy, Oxford, Ohio, and the last doctoral student of Viktor Lowenfeld, at Penn State University. Later, he had invited Schaefer-Simmern to give a lecture at Miami University in late October of 1978, as part of a distinguished art educator lecture series. Unfortunately, Schaefer-Simmern died earlier that same month.
Raymond C. Berta	A Christian Brother and faculty member of Saint Mary's College, Moraga, California, he became interested in the legacy left by Schaefer-Simmern, and chose to do research on the life and work of the latter for his (Berta's) doctoral dissertation, at Stanford University in Palo Alto, California.

A College that Honored Henry Schaefer-Simmern

Henry Schaefer-Simmern, who had taught as a visiting professor at the University of California, in Berkeley, until the fall of 1949, later joined the faculty of Saint Mary's College, in Moraga, California. He received an honorary degree, Doctor of Humane Letters, as Professor Emeritus of Art Education, from this college.

LIST OF FIGURES

Comments and Codes

Every figure (visual example) in this book, with the exception of the color plates, is listed with a brief description in the following list of figures. These entries are acknowledgements of the sources of the many reproductions of pen and ink drawings, photographs and original artworks. The numbers correspond to the figure numbers found in the chapters which are consecutive from 1 to 693. The terms "historic" and "historical" refer not only to historic art, but also to folk art and aboriginal art. The codes in the first column referring to the type of artwork are defined below:

DIAG	Diagram made by the author
DAD	Pen and ink drawing of an adult's drawing
DAP	Pen and Ink drawing of an adult's painting
DCA	Pen and ink drawing reproduction of a child's artwork
DCD	Pen and ink drawing reproduction of a child's drawing
DFA	Pen and ink drawing of folk art
DHR	Pen and ink drawing reproduction of a historical reproduction
OCD	Original child's drawing
PAD	Photograph of a layman adult's drawing
PAP	Photograph of a layman adult's painting
PCD	Photograph of a child's drawing
PCD	Photograph of a child's painting
PHR	Photograph of a historical reproduction
PDHR	Photograph of a pen and ink drawing of a historical reproduction
PHRM	Photograph of a historical original artwork in a museum

Most historical, folk art, and aboriginal art references in the list contain the subject, the name(s) of the author(s), the title of the book in which the reproduction is located, the location and name of the publisher, the date of publication, the page number where the reproduction is located, and the number or letter designation of the figure or plate. The present editors were forced to use whatever data was recorded by the author, the late Professor Henry Schaefer-Simmern, on the back of the mounting sheets of pen and ink reproductions or photographic reproductions of these book reproductions. While he was usually thorough with his recording, here and there some information about a source may be missing and cannot be found and included.

Chapter 1 — From Scribbles to Circular Images

PCD	1	Child, 2 yrs. 6 mon., Nursery School, Frankfurt a/M, 1930.
PCD	2	Child (Claus), 2 yrs. 8 mon.
DHR	3	France, Finger Engraving in Clay of Cave Ceiling, Perch-Merle, about 40,000–30,000 BC.
PCP	4	Girl, 3 yrs. 6 mon., Courtesy: Rhoda Kellogg, Collection, Child Art, San Francisco.
PCD	5	Helen, 3 yrs. 7 mon.
PDHR	6	France, French Pyrenees, about 30–20,000 BC, drawing after H. Breuil, *Four Centuries of Cave Art*, Paris, 1952, Sapho Press, pg. 248, Fig. 268.
PCD	7	Paul, 3 yrs. 6 mon.
PCD	8	Child, 4 yrs.
PDHR	9	USA, Nevada, about 1000 AD, after Heizer, Robert F. & Baumhoff, Martin A., *Prehistoric Rock Art*, Berkeley, CA, 1902, U. of Calif. Press, Plate 813.
PDHR	10	France, Laugerie Haute Dordogne, engraving on pebble, about 15,000 to 10,000 BC, Museum Les Eyzies.
PDHR	11	Italy, Upper Paleolithic, about 20–15,000 BC, (Otranto), drawing after a photograph.
PCD	12	Hannah, 4 yrs. 6 mon.
PCP	13	Esther, 4 yrs. 2 mon.
PCP	14	John, 4 yrs. 7 mon., Courtesy Rhoda Kellogg, Collection, Child Art., S.F., CA.
DHR	15	France, about 10,000 BC, Isturitz, Bone Engraving, after Grazioni, Paulo, *Paleolithic Art*, New York, 1960, McGraw-Hill, Pl. 95.

DHR	16	Ireland, about 2500 BC, Rock Engraving, New Grange, Courtesy: National Monument Branch, Dublin, Ireland, Commissioner of Public Works, Ireland.
DHR	17	N. America, USA, Nevada, 1500 BC – 500 AD, after Heizer, Robert F. & Baumhoff, Martin A., *Prehistoric Rock Art of Nevada and Eastern California*, Berkeley, CA: Univ. of Calif. Press, 1962.
DHR	18	Central Africa, Prehistoric to coming of white man, after Kohl-Larsen, Ludwig, & Kohl, Magrit, *Felsmaleren in inner Africa*, Stuttgart 1928, Stecker und Schöder, Lichtbilder No. 29.
DHR	19	China, Funerary jar, about 2000 BC.
PDHR	20	Egypt, Bowl, 3000 BC.
PCD	21	John, 3 yrs. 6 mon., IAE.
PCD	22	Martin, 3 yrs. 6 mon., German child, IAE.
PCD	23	Franco, 3 yrs. 9 mon., Italian child, IAE.
PCD	24	Joseph, 3 yrs. 6 mon. "That's Me!"
DHR	25	Northern Australia, Rock painting, before coming of white man, to recent times, Courtesy: Frobenious Institute, Frankfurt a/M., Germany.
DHR	26	North America, Nevada,, USA, Rock Engraving, Red Rock Canyon, Wildhorse Spring, Courtesy: Dept. of Anthropology, U. of Calif. Press, Berkeley, CA.
DHR	27	Hawaiian Islands, Puuloa, after 774 AD, after Cox, Halley J., with Stasack, E. *Hawaiian Petroglyphs*, Honululu 1970, Bernice P. Bishop Museum, Fig. 36.
OCD	28	Girl, 3 yrs. 4 mon., Courtesy: Rhoda Kellogg, Child Art Collection, S.F., CA.
OCD	29	Albert, 4 yrs. 2 mon., Courtesy: Kindergarten, Ueberlingen, Germany.
DHR	30	France, about 8000–6000 BC, Painted Pebble, Cave of Mas D'Azil, after Piette, Ed., *Etude D'Etinnographic Pre'Historique*, Paris, 1896, pg. 27, Fig. 36.
DHR	31	Northern Italy, about 1800–1500 BC, Val Camonica, Rock Engraving after Anati, Emmanuele, *La Civilisation Du Val Camonica*, Vichy 1960, Arthud, Plate i.
DHR	32	North America, USA, Nevada, about 1500–1000 BC, Rock Engraving, after Heizer, Robert F. and Baumhoff, Martin A., *Prehistoric Rock Art of Nevada And Eastern California*, Berkeley, CA, 1962, U. of Calif. Press, Pl. 96.
DHR	33	South Africa, Prehistoric Rock Engraving, Driekops Eiland, after: Slack, Lina M. *Rock Engravings from Driekops Eiland*, London 1962, Centavier Press LTD., Pg. 19, Pl. IV.
OCD	34	David, 3 yrs. 4 mon. French Child.
PCD	35	Walter, 6 yrs. 7 mon. German Child.
PCD	36	Ruth, 7 yrs., American Child.
PDHR	37	Japan, 3000–2500 BC, Effigy in fired clay, after Smith, Brealey, *Japan: A History of Art*, 1904, pg. 18.
DHR	38	Crete, 2000 BC Terra Cotta Head, after Bossert, Tk.T., *The Art of Ancient Crete*, London, 1937, Zwemmer. pg. 242, Fig. 423.
DHR	39	Central America, Costa Rica, Head of a Slab Figure, Collection of the author.
DHR	40	N. America, USA, Connecticut, 1728 AD, Head of a gravestone, after Ludwic, Allen, Graven Images, Wesleyan U. Press, 1966, Pl. 224A.
DR	41	Germany, Folk Art, early XIX Cent., Head of a woman, from a Pommeranian Dish, after Harm, Conrad, *Deutsche Volkskunst*, Berlin, 1928, Deutsche Buch-Gemeinschaft, Pl.162.
PCD	42	Nancy, 3 yrs. 5 mon.,"Cat with Kittens."
PCD	43	Paul, 4 yrs. "Many People in a House."
PDHR	44	Spain, Rock Engraving, about 6000–2000 BC.
DHR	45	N. America, California, 2000–1500 BC.
PDHR	46	S. Africa, Prehistoric Rock Engraving, Courtesy: Frobenius Institute, Frankfurt. a/M., Germany.
DHR	47	S. America, Argentina, before white man into 16th cent. AD, Garoner, G. A., *Rock Paintings of North West Cordoba*, Oxford, 1931, At the Clarendon Press, Pl. XXIV.
PCD	48	Martha, 4 yrs.
PCD	49	Donald, Mentally Retarded, 10 yrs., Courtesy: Southbury Training School, Southbury, Connecticut.
DHR	50	Ireland, about 2500–2000 BC, Stone decorated with concentric circles, at Mevagh, after Raftery, Joseph, *Prehistoric Ireland*, London, 1951, Pg. 107, Fig.102.
DHR	51	S. Africa, Courtesy, Frobenius Institute, Frankfurt a/M.,Germany.
DHR	52	N. America, Nevada, about 2000–1500 BC, after Heizer, Robert H. and Baumhoff, Martin A., *Prehistoric Rock Art of Nevada and Eastern California*, Berkeley, CA, U. of Calif. Press, 1962.
DHR	53	Australia, before white man, near the deserted township of Euriowie, after Black, Lindsay, *Aboriginal Art Galleries*, New South Wales, Melbourne 1943, J.Roy Stevens, Pg. 42.

PCP	93	Michael, 4 yrs. 7 mon.,"A Ball with Wheel On" after Tomlinson, R.R., *Children as Artists*, London, & NY, 1947, The Kings Penguin Books.
DHR	94	Crete, about 2000 BC, after Evans, Arthur, Sir, *Scripta Minoa*, Oxford 1909, The Clarendon Press, Pg. 233, Fig. 110.
DHR	95	N. America, USA, Calif. After Von Werlhof, Ray C., Report of the University of California Archaeological Survey No. 65, Berkeley, CA 1965, Dept. of Anthropology, Pg. 87, Fig. 37N.
DHR	96	S. America, Argentina, Late XVI Cent. AD Rock Painting, after Gardner, G.A., *Rock Paintings of Northwest Cordoba*, Oxford 1931, At the Clarendon Press, Pl. XI.
OCD	97	Elsbeth, 4 yrs. 8 mon., "A Flower" IAE.
PCD	98	Clement, 6 yrs. 2 mon., "A Big Turtle" IAE.
PCD	99	Paul, 8 yrs. 9 mon., "A Mouse in a Trap."
PCD	100	Stephen 4 yrs. "A Clown" (Heizer).
DHR	101	Spain, Arco about 10,000–5000 BC Rock Painting "Two Birds in a Magic Circle," after Brodrick, Alan H., *Prehistoric Painting*, London 1948, Avalon Press, Pl. 27.
DHR	102	Egypt, ab. 2900 BC, "Two Oxen in an Enclosure," club head, of King Narmer.
DHR	103	N. America, California, ab. 2000–1500 BC, Rock Engraving, after Von Werlhof, Jay C. *Rock Painting of Owens Valley*, Reports of the U. of Calif. Archaeological Survey No. 65, Dept. of Anthropology, 1965, Pg.58, Fig. 8e.
DHR	104	Northern Spain, ab. 3000–2000 BC, Polvorin near La Coruna, Rock Engraving, after Kühn, Herbert, Die Felsbilder Europas, Stuttgart 1971, Kohlmanner, Pl,55b.
DHR	105	Ireland. about 700 AD, Cross in circular figure, detail from a pillar at Kilnasaggartin, South County, after Henry, Francoise, Irish Art, Ithaca, NY, 1965, Cornell U. Press, Pl.49.
DHR	106	Spain, X Cent AD, "Man Praying with Outstretched Arms," Symbol of prayer circle as a Symbol of the universe, after Demus, Otto,& Hirmer, Max, *Romanische Wandmalerie*, Munich, Germany, 1968, Hirmer Verlag, Pg. 155, Fig. 23.
PDHR	107	France, Late XII Cent. AD, "Sheep of God's Universe," Fresco in St. Aignan-Sur-Cher, Demus, Otto & Hirmer, Max, *Romanische Wandmalerie*, Munich 1968, Hirmer Verlag, Pl. LX.

Chapter 2 — Horizontal-Vertical Line Relationships

PCP	108	Boy, 3 yrs. 5 mon., Courtesy: Rhoda Kellogg, Child Art Collection, San Francisco, CA.
PCD	109	Girl, 4 yrs. 2 mon. Courtesy: Rhoda Kellogg, Child Art Collection, San Francisco, CA.
PCD	110	Girl, 4 yrs. 4 mon. Courtesy: Rhoda Kellogg, Child Art Collection, San Francisco, CA.
DHR	111	South Africa, Rock Engraving, Prehistoric, after Slack, Lina M., *Rock Engravings from Driekop Eiland*, London, 1962, Centaur Press, Pg. 87, Fig. 75.
DHR	112	North America, USA, California, ab. 2000–1500 BC, after Steward, Julian, *Petroglyphs Of California and Adjoining States*, Berkeley, CA, Pl..1. 3ic.
DHR	113	NW Australia, Prehistoric, after McCarthy, Frederick, *The Rock Engravings at Port Hedland, Northwest Australia*, The Kroeber Anthropological Society Papers #26, Univ. of California, Berkeley, CA, Fig. 325f.
DHR	114	Sweden, about 1500 BC, Decorated stone slab from Kivik eist Grave, after Torbrugge, Walter, *Prehistoric European Art*, Harry Abrams, Inc., New York, NY, 1968, Pg. 133.
DHR	115	India, 8000–2500 BC, Rock painting, after Brooks, Robert R. R., *Wakamar, Vishnu Stone Age Paintings of India*, New Haven & London, Yale Univ. Press, Pg. 54.
DHR	116	Jugoslavia, Dalmatia, about XIV Cent., Sun Symbol on a Bogomil Stone, after Rudolf Kutsli, Gampen, Switzerland.
PCD	117	Joe, 4 yrs. 2 mon., Institute of Art Education (IAE), Berkeley, CA.
DHR	118	Child Art, Courtesy: Rhoda Kellogg Nursery School, Child Art Collection, San Francisco.
PCD	119	August, 3 yrs. 11 mon., Frankfurt a/M. Kindergarten, 1956, IAE Collection.
DHR	120	Iberia, Spain, about 2500 BC, Rock Painting, after Breuil, Henri, *Les Peintures Rupestres Schematique De La Peninsule Iberique Ligny*, 1933, Vol. 1, Pg. 20, Fig. 12.
DHR	121	North America, Nevada, about 2000–1000 BC, after Heizer, Robert F. & Baumhoff, Martin A., *Rock Art of Nevada and Eastern California*, Berkeley, CA: Univ. of Calif. Press, 1962, Pg. 247a.
PHR	122	Wampum Circle, Iroquois Indian Art.
OCD	123	Boy, 4 yrs., Courtesy: Rhoda Kellogg, Child Art Collection, *Analysing Children's Art*, National Press Books, Palo Alto, CA 1969, Pg. 109.
OCD	124	Child, 4 yrs., Courtesy: Rhoda Kellogg Child art Collection, *Analysing Children's Art*, National Press Book, 1969, Pg. 83.
DCD	125	Nursery School Child's Drawing, Courtesy Rhoda Kellogg, San Francisco, CA.
DHR	126	S. Africa, Prehistoric, Driekops Eiland (Island) about 1000 yrs. old, after Slack, Lina M., *Rock Engravings from Driekops Eiland*, London 1962, Centauer Press, Pg.80, Fig. 60 (middle right).

PCD	165	Charles, 2 yrs. 1 mon.,"A Railroad Locomotive," after Hildreth, Gertrude, *The Child Mind In Evolution*, New York, NY: King's Crown Press, 1941, Pl. No. I.
PCD	166	Girl, 3 yrs., "Many Legged Man," from Werner, Heinz, *Comparative Psychology of Mental Development*, New York, 1940, Harder and Brothers, Pg. 122.
PCD	167	Child, 3 yrs., 'A Jumping Calf," from Grozner, Wolfgang, *Kinder Kritzeln, Zeichnen, Malen*, Munich, DE: Prestel Verlag, 1952, Pg. 33, Pict. 15.
PCD	168	Claus, 5 yrs., "A Horse."
DHR	169	N. America, California, Owens Valley, about 2000–1500 BC, after Von Werlhof, Jay C. Reports of the University of California Archaeological Survey, No. 65, Berkeley, CA: Dept. of Anthropology, June 1965, Pg. 76, Fig. 266.
DHR	170	China, about 2500 BC, Engraving on a Tortoise Shell.
DHR	171	South Pacific, Prehistoric Petroglyph of the Kei Islands, to our time, after: *The 10thAnnual Report of the of Ethnology*, 1888/89, Washington, D.C. 1893, Pg. 168, Fig. 134.
PCD	172	Ann, 4 yrs., Collection of the Institute of Art Education (IAE), Berkeley, CA.
OCD	173	Boy's Art, 4 yrs. 4 mon., IAE.
OCD	174	Paul, 3 yrs. 6 mon., Kindergarten, Überlingen, Germany.
DHR	175	N. America, Eastern California, about 2000–1500 BC, after Heizer, Robt. F. & Baumhoff, Martin A., *Prehistoric Rock Art of Nevada and Eastern California*, Berkeley, CA: Univ. of Calif. Press, 1902, Pg. 379d.
DHR	176	Italy, Etruscan, Early VI Cent BC, Painted Amphora, after Block, Raymond, Etruscan Art, New York Graphic Society, Greenwich, 1965, Pg. 17, Pl.15.
DHR	177	Asia Minor, Anatolia VI Cent. BC, Hittite Culture, after Pazarli, Whirl from a terra Cotta plaque, round shields of warriors, after *Hittite Art and the Antiqities of Anatolia*, The Art Council, London, A6f, Pg. 137, No. 2.
DHR	178	Japan, VI Cent. AD, Iron Whirl, after a photograph by Keiji Shibata, San Francisco, CA.
PCD	179	Thomas, 4 yrs. 2 mon. "Three People," Collection of IAE.
OCD	180	Berta, 4 yrs. Emerson School, Kindergarten, Teacher: Miss Bank, "Flowers" IAE.
DHR	181	N. America, Nevada, 2000–1500 BC, after Heizer, R. F. & Baumhoff, M.A., *Prehistoric Rock Art of Nevada and Eastern California*, Berkeley, CA: U.of Cal. Press, 1962Plate 5a.
DHR	182	SW Africa, Rock Engraving, after Scherz, Ernst, *Felsbilder in Southwest Africa*, Köln, DE (Germany), and Wein, Austria, 1975, Böhlau Verlag, Pl. 166.
PCP	183	Karl, 5 yrs., Collection of IEA.
PCD	184	Silvia, 7 yrs., IEA.
PCD	185	Martin, 7 yrs., IEA.
PCD	186	Billy, 7 yrs. 8 mon., IEA.
PCD	187	Rosalie, 8 yrs., "A Flower Bed," IEA.
PCD	188	Elizabeth, 6 yrs., "A Woman" IEA.
DHR	189	N. Italy, Istria, Folk Art "Tree" 1815 AD, after an engraved drawing on a horn drinking vessel, Courtesy: Paul Masson Vineyards, Sa n Francisco, CA.
DHR	190	Egypt, detail of a relief carving showing the botanical gardens of Thutmos III, XVIII Dynasty, 1580–1350 BC, from PiJodn, "Summa Artis 3," *Historia General Del Arte*, Pg. 258, Fig. 339.
PCD	191	Child, 5 yrs.,"Tree,"Emerson School, Berkeley, CA, Kindergarten, Teacher: Miss Banks.
PCD	192	Boy, 5 yrs., "tree," Emerson School, Berkeley, CA, Kindergarten, Teacher: Ms. Banks.
OCD	193	Boy, 3 yrs.1 mon., Human Figure, after, Read, Herbert, *Education Through Art*, London, 1943, Faber and Faber, Pg.122.
OCD	194	John, 4 yrs., Courtesy: Emerson School, Berkeley, CA, Kindergarten, Teacher: Ms.Blank.
DHR	195	N. America, California, 2000–1500 BC, after Heizer, R. F. & Baumhoff, M.A., *Prehistoric Rock Art of Nevada and Eastern California*, Berkeley, CA: Univ. of Calif. Press, 1962, Pg. 171, Fig 108b.
DHR	196	Northern Italy, about 900–800 BC, Rock Engraving, after a photograph, Courtesy: Frobenius Institut, Frankfurt a/M., Germany.
DHR	197	S. Africa, after Slack, Lina M., *Rock Engravings from Driekops Eiland*, London, 1962, Centauer Press, Ltd., Pg. 91, Pl. 82.
PCD	198	Gustav, 5 yrs. 7 mon., "2 Big Trees and Smaller Trees."
PCD	199	Donald, 11 yrs. 2 mon., Mentally Retarded Boy, Courtesy: Southbury Training School, Southbury, Connecticut.
DHR	200	Ireland, about 3000–2000 BC, Rock Engraving, after Oriordain, Sean & Daniel, Glyn, New Grange, London, 1964, Thames and Hudson, Pl. 56.

150

DHR   240   Ireland, about 3000–2000 BC, after Raftery, Joseph, *Prehistoric Ireland*, London, 1951, B.T. Batsford, Ltd., Pg. 113.

DHR   241   N. America, California, about 2000–1500 BC, after Steward, Julian H., *Petroglyphs in California and Adjoining States*, Berkeley, CA: Univ. of Calif. Press, 1929, Pg. 77, Fig. 17.

DHR   242   S. Africa, after Slack, Lina, *Rock Engravings from Friekops Eiland*, London 1962, Centaur Press Limited, Pg. 72.

PCD   243   Klaus, 5 yrs.

PCP   244   Ann, 5 yrs. 3 mon.

DHR   245   N. America, Arizona, after Steward, Julian H., *Petroglypha and Pictorgraphs in California and Adjoining States*, Berkeley, CA: Univ. of Calif. Press, 1929, Pg. 162, Fig. 75.

DHR   246   Central Asia, about 2000 BC, North of the Altai River, Figure from a stone pillar, near the Village of Askys, after Applegreen, Kivalo H., *Alt-Altaische Kunst-Denkmäler*, Helsingfors, 1929, Pl. 44, Fig. 217.

DHR   247   Czechoslovakia, about 2000 BC, Figure incised on a pot, after Forman, W. and Poulik, J., *Prehistoric Art*, London, Spring Books, Pl. 26.

PCD   248   Herbert, 5 yrs. 4 mon. "His Small Brother in Bed," IAE Collection, 1949.

DHR   249   Mesopotamia, about 2000 BC, Cylindrical Seal.

DHR   250   Northern Italy, Valcamonica, about 1500–500 BC, after Süss, Emanuele, *Rock Carvings in the Vacamonica*, Milan: Editioni Del Millione, 1954, Pl. 11, No. 13.

PCD   251   Lincoln, 7 yrs., "Dad, Mom, and Me" , Havasupi Indian School, Havasupi Canyon, Arizona 1954.

PCD   252   Girl, 4 yrs. 6 mon., "Dady and Mom," Courtesy: Emerson School, Kindergarten, Teacher: Ms. Bank, 1952.

DHR   253   Egypt, 4th Millenium, BC, after Raphael, Max, *Prehistoric Pottery and Civilization in Egypt*, Bollingier Series VIII, Pantheon Books, Washington, D.C., 1947, PlXXXVI.

DHR   254   France, Burgundy, VII cent. AD, Human figures on a buckle,after Mazenod, M. Lucien, *L'Art Primitif En Suisse*, Geneve: Roto-Sadag S.A., 1942, Pict. No. 3.

DHR   255   Australia, after McCarthy, Frederick, *The Rock Engravings at Port Hedland, Northwestern Australia*, Berkeley, CA: The Kroeber Anthropological Society paper No. 26, University of California, 1962, Fig. 11b,e.

DCD   256   Child, Nursery School, Courtesy: Rhoda Kellogg, Child Art Collection, San Francisco, CA.

PCD   257   Adele, 6 yrs., "A Man in His House."

DHR   258   North America, Nevada, after Heizer, R., & Baumhoff, M., *Prehistoric Rock Art*, Berkeley, CA: Univ. of Calif. Press, 1962, Front Page.

DHR   259   Egypt, Southern Upper Egypt, about 3000 BC, after Winkler, Hans A., *Rock Drawings of Southern Upper Egypt*, II, London: Humphrey Milford, 1939, Pl. XII,2.

PCD   260   Annette, 7 yrs. 2 mon., "My School, My Teacher, and many Kids-Trees in Front of School," Courtesy: Miss Florence Martell, Teacher, Danbury, Connecticut, 1945.

PCD   261   Fred, 8 yrs. "Dady and Mom Picking Apples," Collection of IEA, Berkeley, CA.

PCD   262   Girl, 14 yrs., Mentally Retarded, "Daddy and Mom, I between Daddy and Mom, Johnny, Paul, Doris, and Martha," Courtesy: Southbury Training School, Southbury, Connecticut, 1943, Teacher: Florence Martell.

OCD   263   Eddy, 5 yrs., "A Man." Courtesy: Emerson School, Teacher: Miss Bank, Berkeley, CA.

DHR   264   Greece, about 2500 BC, after Zervos, Christian, *L'Art Des Cyclades*.

DHR   265   Mexico, from Tlatilco State, Late Pre-Classic Culture, about 500–150 BC, drawing after *Official Guide to the Museo National De Anthropologia*, Mexico, 1956, Pl. 5.

DHR   266   Mesopotamia, Sumeria, 3rd Millenium BC, Idol, drawing after Parrot, Andre, *Sumer: The Dawn of Art*, New York, NY: Golden Press, 1961, Pl. XVIII B.

DHR   267   N. America, California, 2000–1500 BC, after Stewart, Julian H., *Petroglyphs in California and Adjoining States*, Berkeley, CA: Univ. of Calif. Press, 1929, Pg. 118, Fig. 46.

DHR   268   North Italy, 900–800 BC.

PCD   269   Daniel, 7 yrs., "Children in the School Yard."

PCP   270   Aileen, 3 yrs. 6 mon., after Alschuler, Rose H. & Weiss Hattwick, LaBerta, *Painting and Personality*, Chicago, IL: Univ. of Chicago Press, 1947, Pl. 7.

PCD   271   Girl, 4 yrs. 6 mon., Courtesy: Johnson Nursery School, Bank Street School, New York City, 1949.

PDHR   272   South America, Peru, 750–800 AD, *Middle Horizon Supe*, Painting on Cloth.

PDHR   273   Persia, Luristan, about 1000 BC, Bronze Figure, after Hudt, Jean-Louis, *Persia I*, Cleveland, OH: The World Publishing Company, 1965, Fig. 87.

Chapter 3 – Variable Line Direction: Trees

PCD   317   Boy, 13 yrs., (Trees and House).

DHR   318   Egypt, 650 BC.

DHR   319   Egypt, 18th Dynasty, 1375–1350 BC.

DHR   320   India, 2nd Quarter of 20th Cent. AD.

DHR   321   India, about 100 BC.

Chapter 4 – Variable Line Direction: the Human Figure

OCD	322	Eve, 5 yrs. 7 mon., Courtesy: Emerson School, Berkeley, CA, 1949.
PCD	323	Boy, 3 yrs. 9 mon.
PCD	324	Girl, 4 yrs.
PCD	325	Boy, 5 yrs. 6 mon., Frankfurt a/M., Germany.
DHR	326	N. America, Nevada, 1500–2000 BC, after Steward, Julian, *Petroglyphs In California and Adjoining States*, Berkeley, CA: Univ. of Calif. Press. 1929.
DHR	327	China, about 3000 BC, after Giles, H. A., *Religion of Ancient China*, London 1905, Pg.14.
DHR	328	Iberia (Spain) about 15000–10,000 BC, Cave of Minateda, after Kühn, Herbert, *On the Track of Prehistoric Man*, New York, NY: 1955, Pg. 145.
DHR	329	N. America, California, about 2000–1500 BC, after Steward, Julian H., *Petroglyphs in California and Adjoining States*, Berkeley, CA: Univ. of Calif. Press, 1929, Pg. 180.
DHR	330	Northern Italy, Valcamonica, about 1500–500 BC, after Süss, Emanuele, *Rock Carvings in the Valcamonica*, Milan, Italy: Edizioni Del Milione, 1954, Pg. 15.
PCD	331	Hannelore, 6 yrs., "Bridal Procession."
PCD	332	Johnny, 7 yrs., "Four Boys."
PCD	333	Margaret, 6 yrs. 2 mon., "Four People."
OCD	334	By a Girl, 10 yrs., "A Boy."
PCD	335	Paul, 4 yrs., "Skating."
PCD	336	Girl, 13 yrs., (Young Woman by Trees).
PCD	337	Eric, 12 yrs., 6 mon. "A Couple Dancing."
PCD	338	Child, 12 yrs., (Basketball Player).
DHR	339	Egypt, Nagada Culture, IV Millenium BC.(or earlier) after a decoration on a bowl, article by Dorner, in *The Evolution of Egyptian Art*, Bulletin of the School of Art, Rhode Island School of Design, July, 1939, Pg. 6.
DHR	340	Northern Italy, Valcomonica, about 1000–500 BC, after Süss, Emanuele, *Rock Carvings of the Valcomonica*, Milan, Italy: Edizioni Del Milione, 1954, Pg. 36.
DHR	341	Japan, about 200 BC to 200 AD, from Kokka, No. 423, Feb. 1926, Back of a Mirror," Pg.45, F.61.
DHR	342	Canada, Late XVIII or early XIX Cent., after a drawing by an Indian on hide, Courtesy: Musee de L'Homme, Paris, France.
DHR	343	France, XI Cent. AD, Roman soldiers, from a scene in the Garden of Gethsemane, Drawing after A capital from the Abbey Church at Saint Pons-De-Thomiers (Herault), after Hammann-MacLean, Richard, *Fruhe Kunst im West Frankischen Reich*, Leipzig, 1939, Pantheon Verlag für Kunst Wissenschaft, Abb. 93.
DHR	344	Italy, Etruscan 470 BC, "Male Dancer," Drawing after a mural painting in the Tomb of the Triclinium at Tarquini, from Skira, Albert, Etruscan Painting, Geneva, 1952, Pg. 76.
OCD	345	Girl, 5 yrs. 4 mon., Emerson School, Berkeley, CA.
DHR	346	Mesopotamia, — Warka, about 3100 BC, after: Moortgat, Anton, *Vorderasiatische Rollsiegel*, Berlin: Verlag Gebr. Mann, 1040, Tafel 4, Fig. 24.
DHR	347	N. America, Nevada, about 2000–1500 BC, Rock Engraving, after Heizer, R. & Baumhoff, M., *Prehistoric Rock Art of Nevada and Eastern California*, Berkeley, CA: Univ. of Calif. Press, Pg.130, Fig. 67.
PCD	348	Boy, 6 yrs. 9 mon. (Animals).
OCD	349	Girl's Drawing, 8 yrs. 2 mon. (2 Animals).
DHR	350	Japan, after a raised line relief on a bronze bell. (4 Animals).
DHR	351	Northern Italy, about 1000–500 BC., Sea Alps, Courtesy: Frobenius Institut, Frankfurt a/M. German.
PCD	352	Girl, 6 yrs. 6 mon. "A Herd of Cattle," Lafayette School, CA, Teacher: Miss Donna Jaidar.
DHR	353	Asia Minor, Troy, about 3000 BC, Engravings on clay pottery, after Schliemann, H., *Troy and Its Remains*, London: John Murray, 1875, Pl. XXIX.

Chapter 5 – Figure – Ground Relationships

PCD	387	Billy, 5 yrs. 2 mon. "A Man," Collection of IEA, Berkeley, CA.
PCP	388	Joan, 6 yrs., "My brother and Me," Collection of IEA, Berkeley, CA.
PCP	389	Child, 7 yrs.
PCD	390	De Ann, 7 yrs., "The Sea Animals," Daughter of Mr. & Mrs. Delman Hague, 1844 Green Valley Rd., Soisun, California 94585.
DHR	391	Mesopotamia – Sumeria, 5th – 4th Millenium BC, after Parrot, Andre, *Sumer, The Dawn of Art*, New York, NY: Golden Press, 1961, Pl. 6.
DHR	392	Peru, 900–1500 AD, after Fuhrman, Ernst, *Peru*, Folkwank ....Pg. 79.
DHR	393	India, 1925–1950 AD, Folk Art Pictograph, From Pandiguda, Ganjam District, Orissa, After Verrier, Elwin, *The Tribal Art of Middle India*, London: Oxford Univ. Press, 1951, opposite Pg. 190.
PCD	394	John, 8 yrs., (6 Horses), Courtesy: Lafayette School, Lafayette, CA, Teacher: Ms. Dona Jaidar, 1962.
PCD	395	John, 8 yrs., (4 horses), Courtesy: (Same as No. 394 above).
PDHR	396	West Australia, XIX Cent. Beagle Bay Mission, Courtesy: De Young Memorial Museum, San Francisco. (Animal Figures, shown with no differentiated ground areas-altered by author to illustrate a point).
PDHR	397	Same as No. 396 above, but after the original, showing differentiated ground areas.
DHR	398	Mesopotamia, 2800–2330 BC, after Porada, Edith, *Mesopotamian Art in Cylinder Seals*, (Shown without Its differentiated ground areas—altered by the author to illustrate a point).
DHR	399	Same as No. 398 Above, but showing the original differentiated ground areas.
DHR	400	Greece, Attic, about 700 BC, Neck of a Funeral Vessel, Courtesy: Museum of Antique Vases, Munich, Germany, (6228).
PDHR	401	Norway, Late XIII Cent., After a detail of a painting from an altar frontal in Odda Church, UNESCO, Pl. XIX.
PCP	402	Boy, 9 yrs. 10 mon., Watercolor Painting , "Clown," Institute of Art Education (IEA) Berkeley, CA.
PCD	403	Emy, 8 yrs. 6 mon. "A Party Under a Big Tree," IEA, Berkeley, CA.
PCD	404	Emy, The same drawing as in Fig. 403, above, but with the tree leaves darkened.
PCD	405	Emy, Same drawing as in Figures 403 and 404, but with the tree completely darkened, some clothing also darkened, and flowers added (serving as base lines for the children).
PCD	406	Emy, Same drawing as in Figure 405, but with many more flowers added.
PCD	407	Kenneth, 13 yrs., Two Soldiers, an outline drawing, Institute of Art Education (IEA) Berkeley, CA.
PCD	408	Kenneth, Same drawing as in Figure 407, above, but with some bushes added.
PCD	409	Kenneth, Same drawing as in Figures 407 and 408 above, but with more bushes and grass added.
PCD	410	Kenneth, Same as in Figure 409, but with earth ground are darkened, and clouds added.
PDHR	411	Ireland, IX Cent., AD., Detail of a cross in Moone-Abbey, County of Kildare, after: Porter, Arthur K. *The Crosses and Culture of Ireland*, New Haven: Yale Univ. Press, 1931, Pl. 115.
PDHR	412	Peru, 1202–1450 AD, Detail of a tapestry, Chancay Style, after Anton, Ferdinand, *The Art of Ancient Peru*, New York, NY: G. R. Putnam's Sons, 1972, Pl. 224.
PDHR	413	Africa, Sudan, Early XIX Cent., After a wooden Panel, Courtesy: Museen Del'Homme, Paris.
DHR	414	Sardinia, 4000–2000 BC., Rock Engravings of Abstract Human Figures, After: Kühn, Herbert, *Die Felsbilder Europas*, Stuttgart & Berlin: Verlag W. Kohlhammer, Pl. 51.
PCD	415	Paula, 8 yrs. 6 mon., "Four Sick People in Bed in a Hospital Room," Courtesy: Grammar School, Lindau, Germany, Teacher: Alfons Handerer.
PCD	416	Girl, 9 yrs., Courtesy: Alfons Handiere Grammar School, Lindau, Germany, Teacher: Alfons Handerer.
DHR	417	Asia Minor, 2000–1700 BC, Cappadocian Cylinder Seal, After: Chariut Scenie, Frankfort, H., *Cylinder Seals*, London: MacMillian & Co. 1939, Pl. XL.
DIAG	418	Figure-Ground Diagram of the Author, Three mountains, outlined and overlapped.
PCP	419	David, 11 yrs., California Hills with Cows and Trees, Courtesy: University of California Elementary School, Berkeley, CA.
PCD	420	Stuart, 10 yrs. 7 mon., "Mountains with Paths, People, Trees, and Goats."
PCP	421	Fred, 12 yrs. 7 mon., "A Tree Covered Hill with a Lookout."
DHR	422	Germany, 1000 AD, "The Lamb of God on the Mountain of Zion," From the Bamberg Apokalypse, After: Wölfflin, Heinrich, *Die Bamberger Apokalypse*, Munich, Germany: Verlag Der Koniglich Bayrischen Akademie Der Wissenschaften, Pl. 34.

Chapter 6 – Spatial Orientations

DHR	531	Crete, about 2500 BC, Seal, A Potter Facing a Shelf with Four Pots, After: Matz, Friedrich, *Die Fruhkretischen Siegel*, Berlin: Verlag von Walter De Gruytier & Co. 1928, Pl. XVII, Fig. 7a.
PCP	532	Susan, 12 yrs., "I Am Taking a Bath," 1959, IEA., Berkeley, CA.
PCD	533	Martin, 10 yrs. 6 mon., "Dinner Table, IEA, Berkeley, CA.
PCD	534	Elizabeth A., 10 yrs. 6 mon. "A Birthday Party," IEA, Berkeley, CA.
PCA	535	Done by 2 Boys, 13 yrs., (outer part) and 12 yrs. (center part), Print, IEA, Berkeley, CA.
PCD	536	Erich, 10 yrs., "On the See-Saw," IEA, Berkeley, CA.
PDHR	537	Scandinavia, Sweden, about 1000–500 BC, Rock Engraving, Two Human Beings Facing Each Other, Courtesy: Frobenius Institut, Frankfurt a/M, Germany.
PCD	538	Simonne, 7 yrs. 7 mon. Drawing "Horse with Cart," From: C. Luquet, *Les Dessing D'un Enfant*, Paris: Pg. 172 et seg.
PCD	539	Karin, 9 yrs., "A Wagon Full of Stones with Two Horses," IEA, Berkeley, CA.
DHR	540	Sweden, 1000–500 BC, Gotland Rock Engraving, After: Christiansen, Erwin O., *Primitive Art*, New York, NY: Thomas Y. Crowell & Co., Pg. No. 49.
DHR	541	Italy, about 900–700 BC, Rock Engraving, in the Val Camonica, After: Anati, Emmanuel, *La Civilisation Du Val Camonica*, Vichy, France: Les Presses De L'Imprimerie Wallon, 1960, Pg. 15.
PDHR	542	North Africa, 1 – 100 AD, After: Frobenius, Leo, *Das Urbild*, Frankfurt a/Main, Germany: Forschungs Institut für Kulturmorphologie, Pg. 55.
PCD	543	Fritz H., 9 yrs., "Wagon Loaded with Sacks of Potatoes," 1932, Institute of Art Education.
DHR	544	Italy, about 900–700 BC, in the Val Camonica, After Anati, Emmanuel, *La Civilisation Du Val Camonica*.
DHR	545	Sweden, about 1200 BC, Carved, Two Wheeled Chariot Carved on a Stone Slab, At a tomb at Kivik.
PDHR	546	North Germany, (Prussia) about 500–400 BC, Incised in an urn of clay. Horses Pulling a Wagon.
DHR	547	North East Germany (West Prussia), about 600 BC, Horses Pulling a Wagon or Plow, Scratched on an Urn, After: Hoernes, M., *Urgeschichte Der Bildenden Kuns in Europa*, Wien: Anton Schroll & Co., 1915, Page 529.
PCD	548	Karin, 12 yrs. 6 mon., "Swimming Pool with Two Swimmers and Children," IEA, Berkeley, CA.
PDHR	549	Egypt, about 1500 BC., Garden Scene, after a mural painting, Courtesy: The Metropolitan Museum Of Art, New York City, NY.
DHR	550	Persia, 1398 AD., Detail of a Persian Miniature Painting, Courtesy: Of the Late Mr. Mehnet Aga, NY.
DCD	551	Girl, 8 yrs. 7 mon., "The Party," (Showing a tendency toward a total relationship of all figures.) A copy Of a child's drawing done by the author. Institute of Art Education, Berkeley, CA.
DHR	552	Italy, XI Cent. AD, After a bronze Plaque of the Door of the Church of St. Zeno, in Verona, "Christ in Limbo," Photograph Lore Hamacher, Konstanz, Germany.
DHR	553	Mesopotamia, 669–626 BC, Time of King Ashurbanipal, After a detail of a relief: The Defeat of the From: Frankfort, Henry, *The Art and Architecture of the Ancient Orient*, London: Penguin Books, 1954, P.2. 103.
PHR	554	Turkey, 1398 AD, Detail of a Mystical Landscape, After: Ipsiroglu, M. S., *Das Bild Im Islam*, Wien: Verlag Anton Schroll & Co., 1971, Frontpiece.
PCA	555	Cooperative Mural Painting, Done by Boys and Girls, 8, 9, and 10 yrs. of age, "Passover Seder" San Francisco Jewish Community center, Arts and Crafts Class, 1956, San Francisco, CA.
PCP	556	A Cooperative Work by two Boys, 12 yrs. of age, "A Park Scene."
PDHR	557	Egypt, About 1400 BC, "Garden with Pool," After: A Mural Painting in Tomb No. 85, Amenemhab, Thurmosis III – Amenophis II, 1447–1375 BC, Courtesy; Uni-Dias-Verlag, Grosshesse Lohe, Germany.
PCD	558	Roy, 7 yrs. 2 mon., "An Orchard," Institute of At Education (IEA), Berkeley, CA.
PCD	559	Elsa, 6 yrs. 5 mon., "Two Dogs," IEA, Berkeley, CA.
OCD	560	Berta, 12 yrs. 6 mon., "Children Playing," IEA, Berkeley, CA.
PCP	561	Erich, 13 yrs., Landscape wit Three Trees, IEA, Berkeley, CA.
PAP	562	Drawing by a 56 year old Layman, "Cactus Garden."
DHR	563	Persia, 1315 AD, Miniature painting: The Ming Sons of Tu Lu Khan, Courtesy: The Metropolitan Museum of Art, New York City, New York.
DHR	564	Switzerland, 2nd Half of the 19th Cent., AD, After an illumination from the Codex St. Gallen.
PDHR	565	India, End of XVIII Cent., Drawing after an Indian Miniature, "Polo Game," After: Orbis Pictus, *Indische Miniaturen Der Islamischen Zeit*, Berlin: Verlag Ernst Wasmuth A. G., 1921, Pl. 17.

Chapter 7 – Spatial Depections

DHR	601	Greece, Early 10th Cent. AD., Detail from a Book Illustration, After Grabar, Andre, *Byzantine Painting*, Geneva: Albert Skira, 1953, Fig. 168.
DHR	602	Constantinople, 1285 AD., Foot Stool, Detail of a miniature, from the *Gospel Book, St. Luke, Collex Burney* 20, London: Courtesy: British Museum.
PCD	603	Boy, 13 yrs., "Our Dining Room," IEA, Berkeley, CA.
DHR	604	China, Six Dynasties, 220–589 AD, Simplified drawing of a fortified monastery, on a wall painting Cave 296,, Tunhuang, After: Sullivan, Michael, *The Birth of Landscape Painting in China*, Berkeley, CA: Univ. of Calif. Press, 1962, Pl. 119.
PDHR	605	Italy, Rome, Early 1st cent. AD, Drawing after a mural painting. Courtesy: The Metropolitan Museum of Art, New York City, NY.
DHR	606	India, 18th Cent. AD, Simplified drawing after a detail in a Kangra Valley painting, From: The Publication Division, Ministry of Information and Broadcasting, of India, Pl. 23.
DHR	607	Italy, 15th Cent., Drawing after an engraving by Laserentius De Voltolina, Lecture of Henricus De Alemania, University of Bologna.
PCD	608	Richard, 12 yrs. 6 mon., "Playing Chess with My Father," IEA, Berkeley, CA.
PCD	609	Drawing by a Boy, 13 yrs., (Drawing Class)., IEA, Berkeley, CA.
PCD	610	Paul, 13 yrs. 8 mon., "I am Getting Up," IEA, Berkeley, CA.
PCD	611	Drawing by Eric Stolz, 9 yrs., "Family on a Bench," IEA, Berkeley, CA.
DHR	612	China, Simplified drawing of a temple complex.
DHR	613	Italy, About 1300 AD, After a building in a painting by Ducio (1255–1310 AD), "Temptation of Christ."
PCD	614	Kenneth, 13 yrs. 6 mon., Drawing, "A Small Town," IEA, Berkeley, CA.
PCD	615	Boy, 13 yrs. 6 mon., Drawing, "An Airplane over a Small Town," IEA, Berkeley, CA.
DHR	616	Mexico, 1628 AD, Drawing after a detail from a map entitled: "Forma Y Levantado De La Ciudad, Ciudad De Mexico, Published in Florence, Lithograph A Ruffoni, Courtesy: Nabcroft Library, University of California, Berkeley, CA.

Chapter 8 — Development of Face and Eye

PCD	617	Carda, 6 yrs., Überlingen, Germany, Kindergarten, Courtesy: Miss Traute Pause-Back, Teacher.
PDHR	618	N. America, Massachusetts, 1717 AD, Head from a Hanah Johnson's Grave Stone, Rowley, Mass., After: Ludwig, Allen A., *Graven Images*, Middletown, Connecticut: Wesleyan Univ. Press, 1966, Pl. 221c.
PDHR	619	India, 1962 AD, Head from a Grave Stone, After: Archer, W. G., *The Vertical Man*, London: George Allen Unwin, 1947, Pl. 25.
PCD	620	Leni, 12 yrs., Institute of Art Education, IEA, Berkeley, CA.
PDHR	621	Greece, VI Cent., BC., After Zervos, Christian, *L'Art En Greece*, Paris: Edition Cahier D'Art, 1926, Pl. 113.
PDHR	622	France, XII Cent., AD, After: Focillon, Henri, *Painture Romans Des Eglises De France*, Paris: Edition Paul Hartmann, Pg. 43, Fig. 1.
PDHR	623	Ethiopia, 1434–1468 AD, Head of an Angel, From an Annunciation Gospel of the Emperor Zara Yacob.
PDHR	624	Africa, XIX Cent. AD, Ivory Coast, Drawing after a Mask in the collection of the author, Berkeley, CA.
PCP	625	Martin, 7 yrs. 6 mon. "My Friend." IEA, Berkeley, CA.
PCD	626	Elise, German Girl, 8 yrs., "My Mother," IEA Collection, Berkeley, CA.
DHR	627	France, III Cent, AD., After a Mask in the Museum of Tarbes-Haute Pyrenes.
DHR	628	Germany, about 1400 AD, Head of an Abbot from a tombstone in the Abbey Church of Mittelzell, on the Island of Reichenau, After a photograph by Lore Hamacher, Schopfheim, Germany.
DHR	629	India, XIX Cent., AD., Folk Art, Majhiyawan District Gaya, Head of a flat stone sculpture, After: Archer, W. G., *The Vertical Man*, London; George Allen and Unwin, Ltd., 1947, Pl. 7.
PCD	630	Ruth, 7 yrs., (Girl), IEA, Berkeley, CA.
PCD	631	Fred, 10 yrs. 6 mon, "Dad, Mom and Me," IEA, Berkeley, CA.
DHR	632	Palestine, Jordan Valley, about 7000 BC, Head of a Yarmukian Clay Figure, After: Mellaart, James, *Earliest Civilization of the Near East*, New York, NY: McGraw Hill Book Comp., 1965, Pg.61,Fig. 37.
DHR	633	Greece, about 2000 BC, After: Blegen, Carl W., *Zygouries: A Prehistoric Settlement in the Valley of Cleonae*, Cambridge, Massachusetts: Harvard Univ. Press, 1928, Pl. 21.1.
DHR	634	Mexico, 300 BC – 300 AD., Chupicuaro Clay Figure, Courtesy: Edgar D. Taylor, Los Angeles, CA.

PCD	671	Boy, 12 yrs., IEA, Berkeley, CA.
PCD	672	Boy, 14 yrs. 2 mon., IEA, Berkeley, CA.
DHR	673	England, about 750 AD, Head from a miniature of the Evangeliar, from Lindisfarne, From: Zimmermann, E.H. *Vorkarolingische Miniaturen Vol. III*, Berlin: Deutscher Verein Für Kunstwissenschaft, 1916, Ta.
DHR	674	France, 12th cent. AD, Drawing after a detail of a fresco in the Church of Saint Martin-De-Vic, in the Bourbonnais, From: Ainaud, Juan & Held, Andre, New York, NY: The Viking Press, 1963, Pl. 68.
DHR	675	Austria-Tirol, about 15th Cent. AD, After a carving in a wooden board, Courtesy: Tirolean Folk- Museum, Innsbruck, Austria.
PCD	676	Ann, 11 yrs., "The Head of a Dog," Institute of Art Education, Berkeley, CA.
DHR	677	Greece, about 500 BC, Lake Trotp, Corinth, Drawing after Pottery, B.S.A., Vol. 48, Pl. 61.
DHR	678	Greece, XI Cent. BC., After: Feligietti, – & Liebenfels, Walter, *Geschichte Der Byzantinischen Ikonenmalerei*, Olten a Lausanne: Urs-Graf-Verlag, 1956, Pl. 11A.
DHR	679	Norway, XIII Cent AD, Detail of an altar canopy, From Ardal Church in Sogn, After: Hauglid, Roar, & Grodecki,, Louis, Norway: *Paintings from the Stave Churches*, Paris: UNESCO, 1955, Pl. XIII.
DHR	680	Russia, 1408–1425 AD, Ikon of Apostle Paul, After: Ouspensky, Leonid, & Lossky, Wladimir, *Der Sinn Der Ikonen*, Bern, Switzerland: Urs-Graf-Verlag, 1953, Pg. 113.
OCD	681	Virginia, 14 yrs. 6 mon., "My Friend."
DHR	682	Mexico, 672 AD, Detail from a Stone Tablet, After: Groth-Kimball, Irmgard, & Feuchtwanger, Franz, *The Art of Ancient Mexico*, London: Thames and Hudson, 1954, Pl. 48.
OCD	683	Alice, 14 yrs., (Girl's Head), IEA, Berkeley, CA.
PHRM	684	India, XVIII Cent. D., After a Miniature, Courtesy: the Metropolitan Museum of Art, New York City, NY.
PHR	685	Sweden, 1848 AD, After Svädström, Svante, *Masterieces of Dala Peasant Paintings*, Stockholm: Albert Bonniers Förlag, 1957, Cover Image.
PAD	686	Drawing by a Woman, of a Woman's Head, 47 yrs. of age, IEA, Berkeley, CA.
PCD	687	Nina, 15 yrs., Head of a Girl, IEA, Berkeley, CA.
DHR	688	Greece, Late VI Cent. BC, Head, From a vase Painting by "The Berin Painter," After: Arias, Paolo Enrico, & Hirmer, Max, *Tuasend Jahre Griechische Vasenmalerei*, Munich, Germany: Hirmer Verlag, 1960, Pl. 155.
DHR	689	Greece, 440 BC, Head of Achilleus, from an Amphora, Vatican City Museo Gregoria-No. Etrusco, After: Arias, P.E., & Hirmer, M., *Tausend Jahre Griesche Vasenkunst*, Munich Germany: Hirmer Verlag, 1960, Pl. XL.
PHRM	690	India, Late VIII Cent. AD, Detail after an Indian Miniature, Courtesy: The Metropolitan Museum of Art, New York City, NY.
PCD	691	Nina, 16 yrs., "Self Portrait," Pencil Drawing, IEA, Berkeley, CA.
PCD	692	Deborah, 18 yrs., Portrait of a Young Man, Pencil Drawing, IEA, Berkeley, CA.
PCD	693	Charry, 17 yrs., Portrait of a Girl, Pen & Ink Drawing, IEA, Berkeley, CA.

REFERENCES

This reference list consists of those books and periodicals which the editors know were used by the late author, Henry Schaefer-Simmern. Many other references that he used in his research are to be found in the extensive List of Figures.

Books

Arnheim, R.	*Art and Visual Perception*. Berkeley, CA: The University of California Press, 1954.
Britsch, G.	(1966, 4th ed.). *Theorie der bildenden Kunst*. Ratingen, Germany: Aloys Henn Verlag, 1926.
Dewey, J.	(1948), Foreword, *The unfolding of Artistic Activity*. Berkeley, CA: The University of California Press, pp. ix-x.
	(1958), *Art as Experience*. New York, NY: Capricorn Books, G. P. Putnam's Sons.
Fiedler, C.	(1957, 2nd ed.), On *Judging works of Visual Art*. (trans.) Schaefer-Simmern, H., Mood, f., Berkeley, CA: The University of California Press, 1st ed. 1949.
Herrmann, H.	(1963), *Zeichnen fürs Leben*. Ratingen, Germany: A. Henn Verlag.
Kellogg, R.	(1966), Stages of development in preschool art, *Child Art: the Beginnings of Self-affirmation*. Berkeley, CA: The Diablo Press, pp. 27-31, 42-43.
Kellogg, R. & O'Dell, S.	(1967), *The Psychology of Children's Art*. A Psychology Today Book, CRM-Random House Publication.
Kornmann, E.	(1962), *Grundprinzipien Bildnerischer Gestaltung*. Ratingen, Germany: A. Henn Verlag.
Kornmann, L.	(1952), *Leben und Werk von Gustaf Britsch*. Ratingen, Germany: Aloys Henn Verlag.
Read, H.	(1955), *Icon and idea*. Cambridge, MA: Harvard University Press.
	(1960), *The Forms of Things Unknown*. Cleveland, OH: Meridian Books: the World Publishing Company.
Sarason, S.	(1949), *Psychological Problems in Mental Deficiency*. New York, NY: Harper & Brothers.
	(1985), *Psychological & Mental Retardation: Perspectives in Change*. Austin, TX: pro-Ed, Inc.
Schaefer-Simmern, H.	(1948), *Unfolding of Artistic Activity*. Berkeley, CA: The University of California Press.

Periodicals

Herrmann, H. (ed.)	*Die Gestalt*, Ratingen, Germany: Aloys Henn Verlag, issues: 1951-1968
Abrahamson, R.	(1989). Henry Schaefer-Simmern: His life and works. *Art Education*, 33 (8), December, 12-16.